ASSESS YOUR IQ

ASSESS YOUR IQ

Numerical, Verbal and Spatial Aptitude Tests

Philip Carter & Ken Russell

KoganPage

LONDON PHILADELPHIA NEW DELHI

First published in 2003 as The Times Book of IQ Tests, book 3 by Kogan Page Limited

Reissued in 2012 as *Assess Your IQ*

Kogan Page Limited
120 Pentonville Road
London N1 9JN
UK
www.koganpage.com

1518 Walnut Street, Suite 1100
Philadelphia PA 19102
USA

ISBN 978 0 7494 6679 4

British Library Cataloguing-in-Publication Data

A CIP record for this book is available from the British Library.

Typeset by Saxon Graphics Ltd, Derby
Printed and bound in India by Replika Press Pvt Ltd

Contents

Introduction

Intelligence quotient (IQ) is an age-related measure of intelligence level and is defined as 100 times the mental age. The word quotient means the results of dividing one quantity by another, and intelligence can be defined as *mental ability* or *quickness of mind*.

An intelligence test (IQ test) is, by definition, any test that purports to measure intelligence. Generally, such tests consist of a graded series of tasks, each of which has been standardized with a large representative population of individuals. Such procedure establishes the average IQ as 100.

IQ tests are part of what is generally referred to as Psychological Testing. Such test content may be addressed to almost any aspect of our intellectual or emotional make-up, including personality, attitude, intelligence or emotion. In different parts of the world a wide range of such tests are in use. These include Achievement Tests, which are designed to assess performance in an academic area; Aptitude Tests, which predict future performance in an area in which the individual is not already trained; Objective Personality Tests, which are designed to provide an overall profile of the personality of the individual being assessed, and Intelligence (IQ) Tests.

The earliest known attempts to rank people in terms of intelligence date back to the Chinese Mandarin system, *c*. 500 BC, when studying the works of Confucius enabled successful candidates to enter the public service. The top 1 per cent of candidates were successful in progressing to the next stage, where they would again be run off against each other, and the procedure repeated yet again through a final layer of selection. Thus, the chosen candidates were in the top 1 per cent of the top 1 per cent of the top 1 per cent.

The first modern intelligence test was devised in 1905 by the French psychologists Alfred Binet and Theodore Simon. The pair developed a 30-item test with the purpose of ensuring that no child be denied admittance to the Paris school system without formal examination.

In 1916, the American psychologist Lewis Terman revised the Binet-Simon scale to provide comparison standards for Americans from age three to adulthood. Terman devised the term *intelligence quotient* and developed the so-called Stanford-Binet intelligence test to measure IQ after joining the faculty of Stanford University as professor of education. The Stanford-Binet test was further revised in 1937 and 1960 and remains today one of the most widely used of all intelligence tests.

It is generally believed that a person's IQ rating is hereditary and that a person's mental age remains constant in development to about the age of 13, after which it is shown to slow up; and beyond the age of 18 little or no improvement is found.

When measuring the IQ of a child, the subject will attempt an IQ test that has been standardized with an average score recorded for each age group. Thus, a child of 10 years of age who scored the results expected of a child of 12 would have an IQ of 120, calculated as follows:

mental age (12)/chronological age (10) × 100 = 120 IQ

However, because in adulthood little or no improvement in IQ rating is found, adults have to be judged on an IQ test whose average score is 100 and their results graded above and below this norm according to known scores.

During the past 25–30 years IQ testing has been brought into widespread use by employers because of their need to ensure they place the right people in the right job from the outset. One of the main reasons for this in today's world of tight purse strings, cost-cutting and low budgets is the high cost of errors in employing the wrong person for a job, including the need to readvertise and interview new applicants, and reinvestment in training.

Because IQ is hereditary, it is not, therefore, possible to increase your actual IQ. It is, however, possible to improve your performance in IQ tests by practising the many different types of question, and learning to recognize the recurring themes. The questions in this book are typical of the type and style of question you are likely to encounter in actual tests and are designed to provide valuable practice for anyone who may have to take this type of test in the future. It is our belief that by practising on different types of IQ tests, and by getting your mind attuned to the different types of questions you may encounter, and the thought processes necessary to solve many of them, it is possible to improve by a few vital percentage points. It is these few percentage points that may prove crucial in increasing your job prospects and mean the difference between success and failure when attending one of the many job interviews that include the taking of an IQ test.

The tests that follow have been newly compiled for this book and are not, therefore, standardized, so an actual IQ assessment cannot be given. However, there is a guide below to assessing your performance at the end of one test, and there is a cumulative guide for your overall performance on all 10 tests.

A time limit of *90 minutes* is allowed for each test. The correct answers are given at the end of each test, and you should award yourself one point for each correct answer. Calculators may be used to assist with solving numerical questions if preferred. Use the following table to assess your performance:

One test

Score	*Rating*
36–40	Exceptional
31–35	Excellent
25–30	Very good
19–24	Good
14–18	Average

Ten tests

Score	*Rating*
351–400	Exceptional
301–350	Excellent
241–300	Very good
181–240	Good
140–180	Average

It should be pointed out that intelligence tests only measure one's ability to reason, they do not measure the other qualities that are required for success such as character, personality, talent, persistence and application.

A person with a high IQ has a better chance of success in life than a person with a low IQ, but only if that person applies his or herself to the tasks ahead diligently and with enthusiasm. Someone with a relatively low IQ but with a high sense of achievement and great persistence can fare better in life than someone with a high measured IQ.

Cynics will say that the only thing having a high IQ proves is that the individual has scored well on an intelligence test. An IQ test, however, remains the only known and tried method of measuring intelligence. Some technical weaknesses do exist, and because of this it is crucial that results be viewed as only one kind of information about an individual. Nevertheless, it must be stressed how commonplace IQ tests have become, and that proficiency at IQ tests can improve one's employment prospects and give a good start to one's chosen career.

Test One: Questions

1. 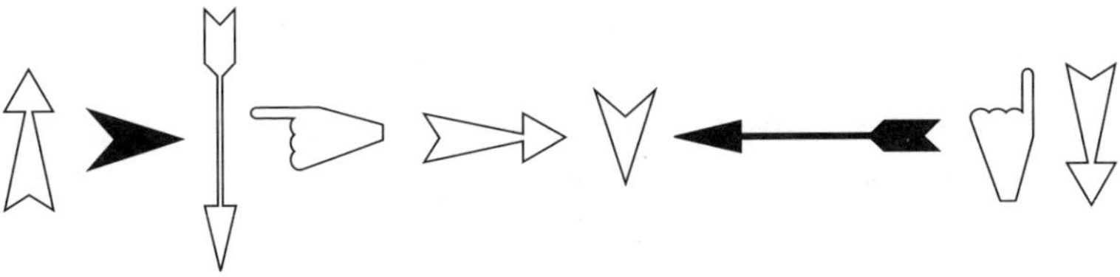

Which two arrows come next?

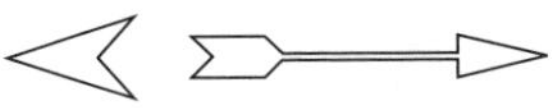

A

B

C

D

E

F

2. PIANIST RULES is an anagram of which two words that are opposite in meaning?

3. Work from letter to adjacent letter, horizontally, vertically or diagonally to spell out a 12-letter word. You must find the starting point and provide the missing letters.

   I T S *

   A L O O

   N C O *

4. How many minutes is it before 12 noon if 16 minutes ago it was three times as many minutes after 9 am?

5.

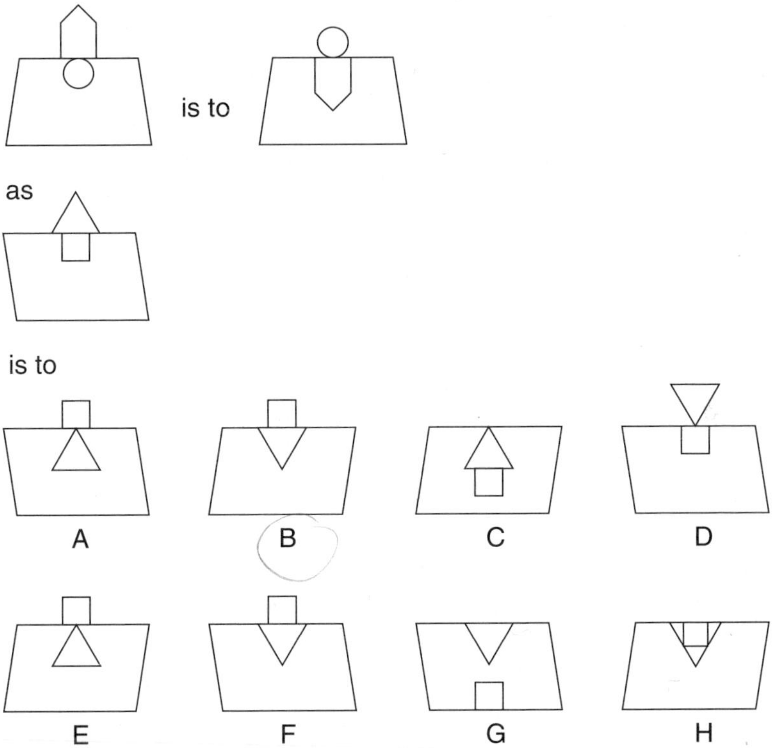

6. Which is the odd one out?

vixen, vulpine, reynard, lupine, brush

7. Which word can be placed in the brackets that has the same meaning as the words either side of the brackets?

ARMADA (– – – – –) SWIFT

9. 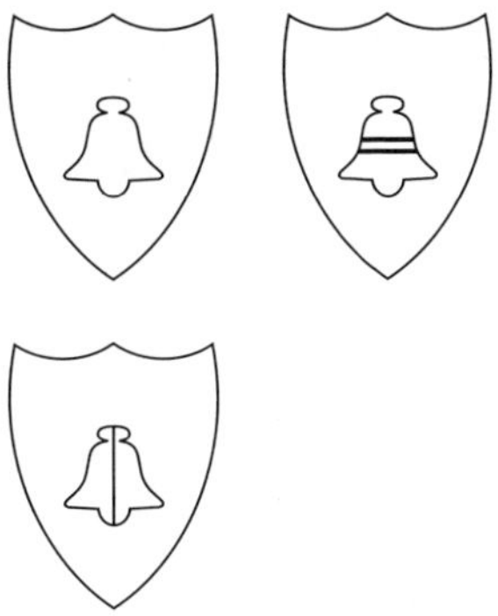

Which is the missing shield?

A B C D E

10. Beaufort is to wind as Munsell is to:

music, colour, minerals, weight, intelligence

11. Solve the cryptic clue. The answer is a nine-letter word anagram within the clue:

wise bands deteriorate into lasciviousnes

12. 64521 is to 41256 as 38297 is to:

a. 89732; b. 29873;

c. 92837; d. 87923;

e. 87932.

13. How many lines appear below?

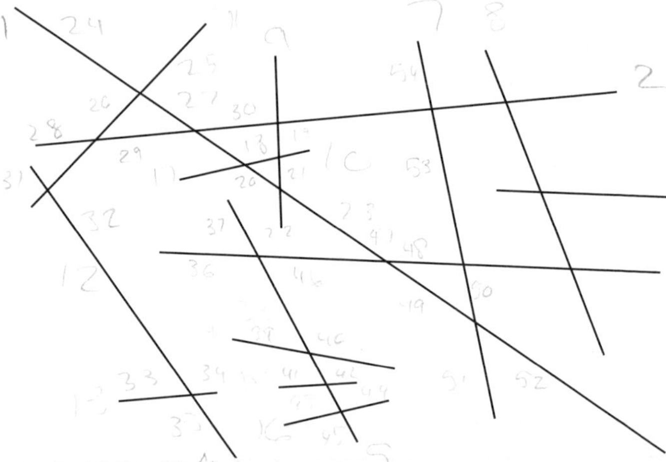

14. Complete the two eight-letter words that are synonyms, one reading clockwise and the other anticlockwise. In each word, you must provide the missing letters and find the starting points.

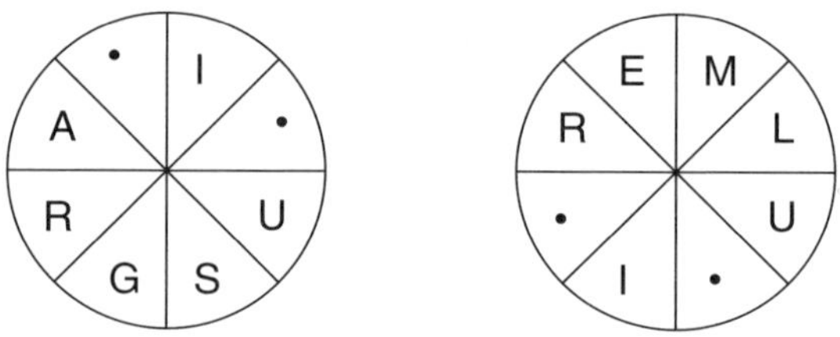

15. Find a word that when tacked onto the end of the first word produces another word or phrase and when placed in front of the second word produces another word or phrase.

BONE (– – – – –) TOWN

16. What number comes next in this sequence?

1, 3, 11, 47, ?

17.

Which is the missing segment?

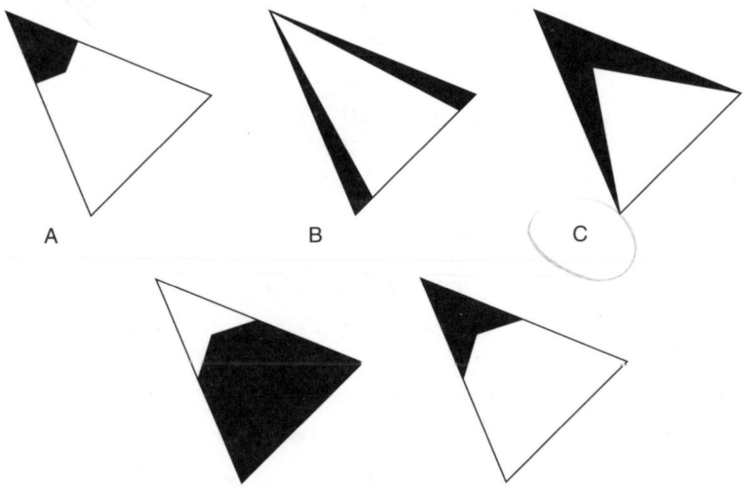

A B C

D E

18. Change one letter only in each word to produce a familiar phrase:

    go hit us

19. What number comes next in this sequence?

    100, 97.25, 91.75, 83.5, ?

20. Which is the odd one out?

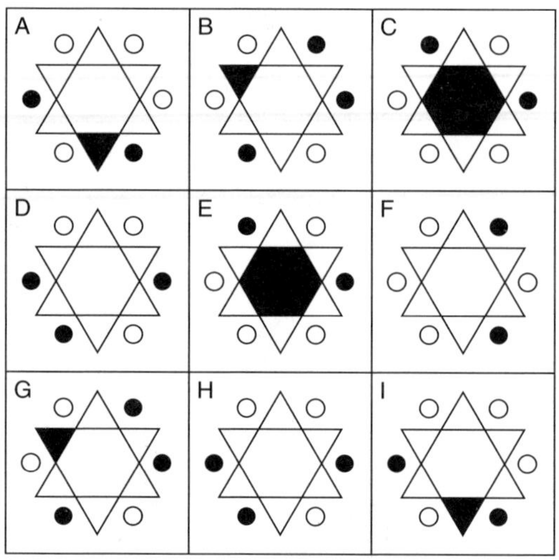

21. All of the vowels have been omitted in this trite saying. See if you can replace them.

    YCNNT TLLHW DPPDD LSNTL YSTPN T

22.

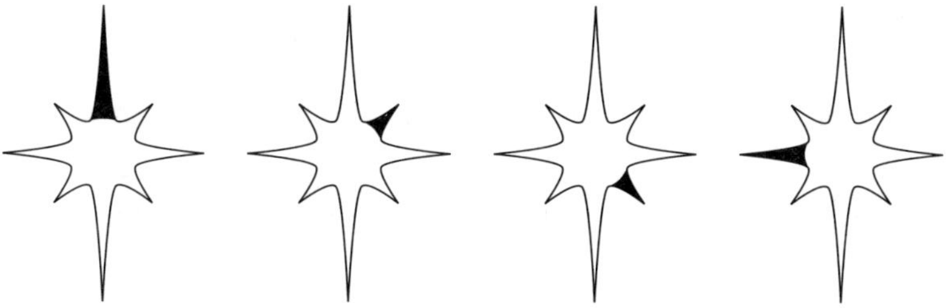

What comes next?

A

B

C

D

E

F

G

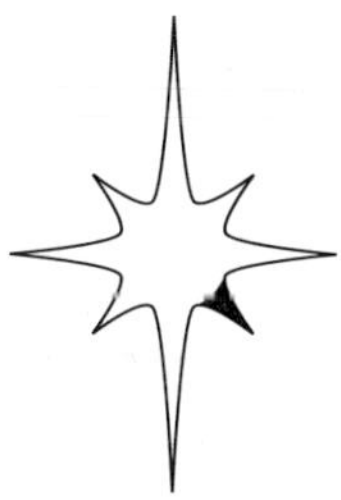

H

23. Identify a number in the grid that meets the two following simple rules:

    a. It is not in any line across that contains a square.

    b. It is not in any line down that contains a prime number.

23	36	8	48
7	6	13	16
15	21	3	5
18	25	4	12

24. Fill in the blanks to find a MINERAL clockwise or anticlockwise.

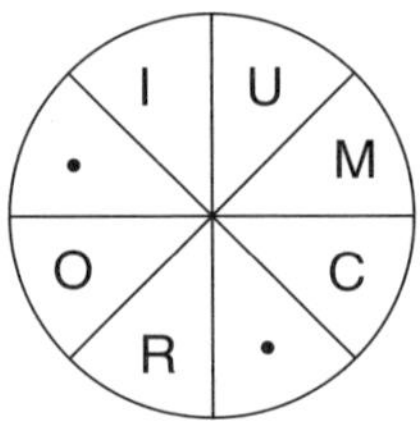

25. Insert a word that completes the first word and starts the second word.

    CHIMNEY (– – – – –) STAKE

26. Insert a word inside the brackets that means the same as the words outside the brackets.

    SEIZE EAGERLY (– – – – – –) SET OF EGGS

27. What is a SAMOYED?

    a. a flat raft;

    b. an Arctic breed of dog;

    c. a leather belt;

    d. a Russian teapot;

    e. a small cooking stove.

28. Spell out a 10-letter word by visiting the circles only once.

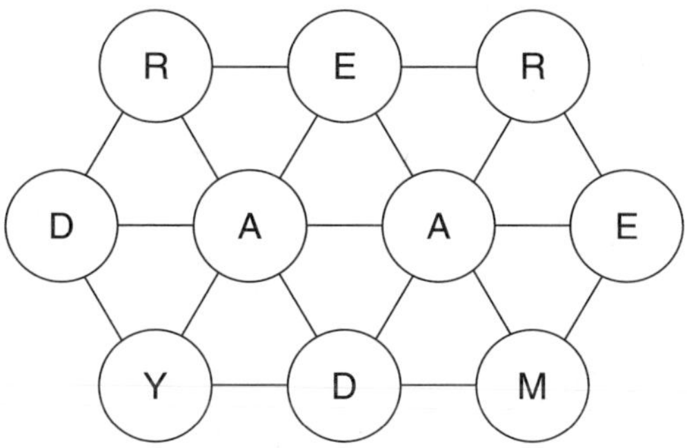

29.

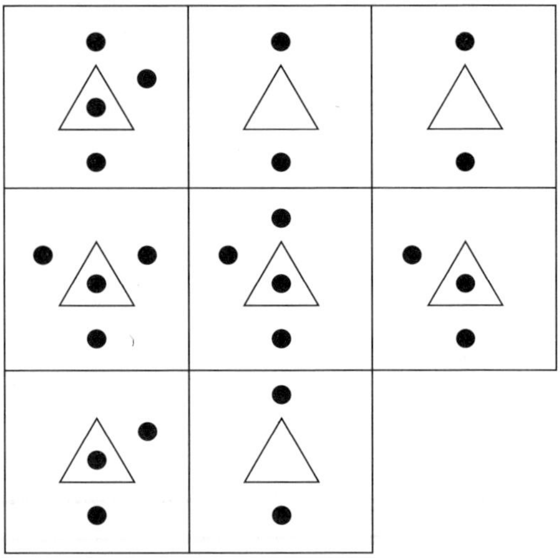

Which is the missing square?

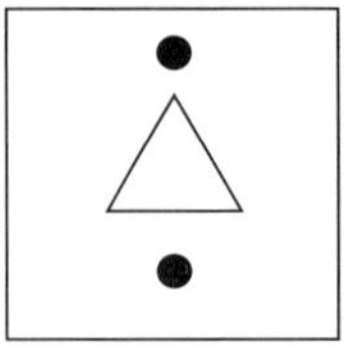

A

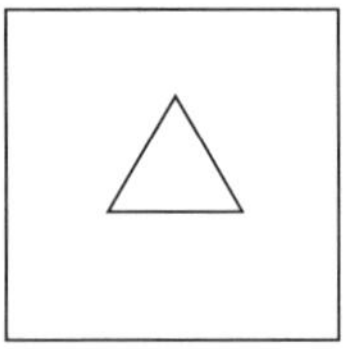

B

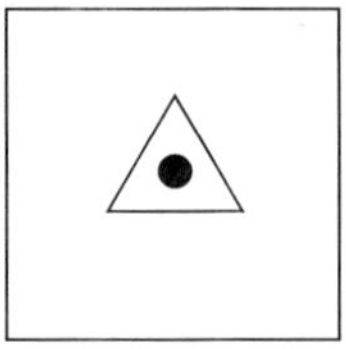

C

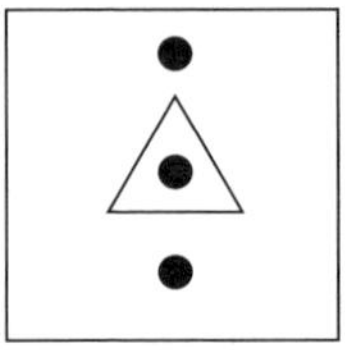

D

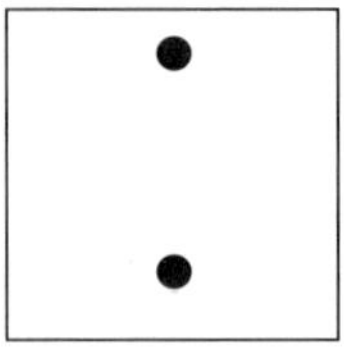

E

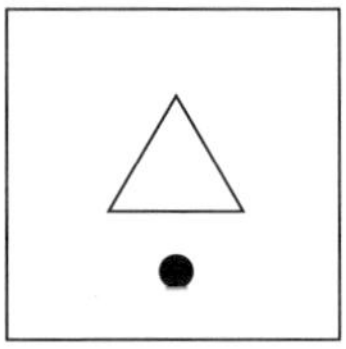

F

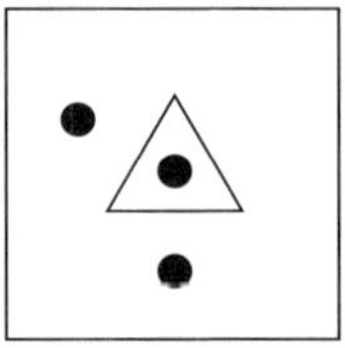

G

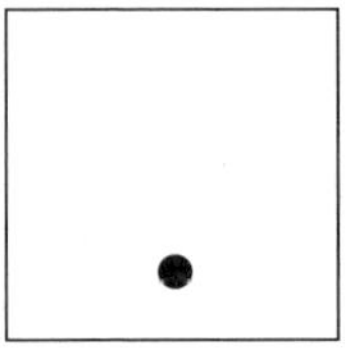

H

30. Letters are traced across the circle by chords. If the next letter is four letters or less away it will be found by tracing around the circumference.

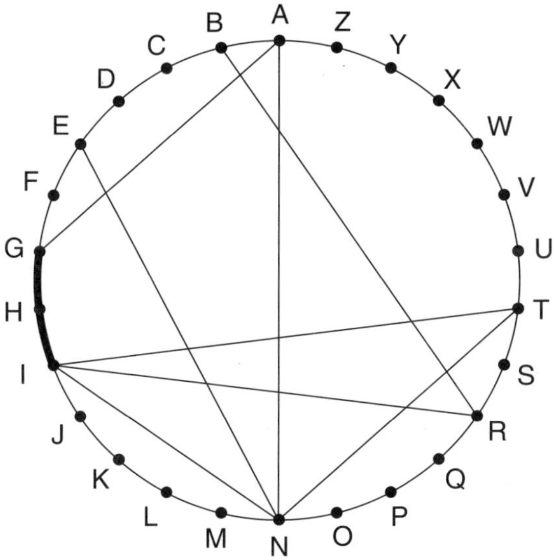

Clue: ANCIENT SHIP (10 letters)

31. Which word means the same as SOPORIFIC?

a. jumpy;

b. insufficient;

c. fragrant;

d. narcotic?

32. Find a one-word anagram for:

RICHARD HOPS

33. Place three two-letter bits together to equal a MARINE GROWTH.

DE MP IA

ET LI NA

34.

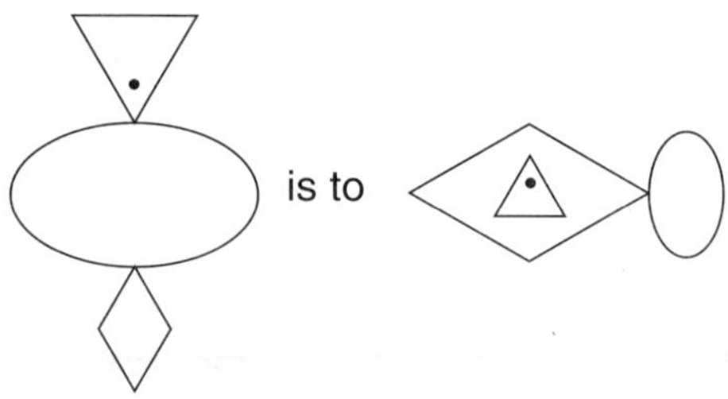

as

is to

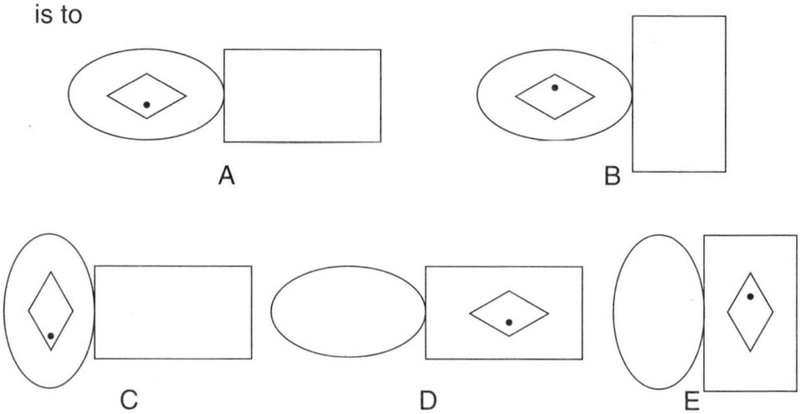

35. What number should replace the question mark?

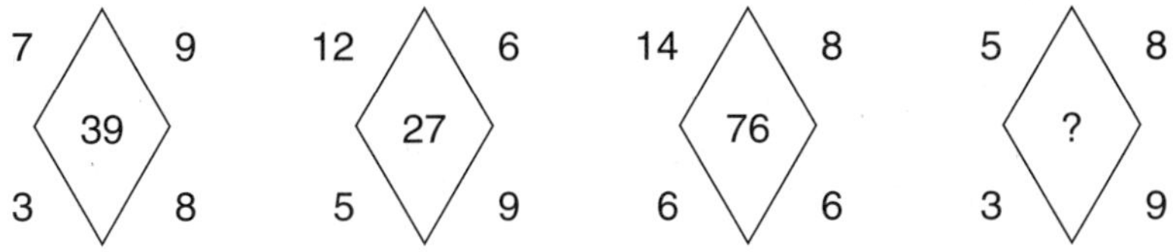

36. Insert a word that completes the first word and starts the second word.

SHOOTING (– – – –) DUST

37. What number should replace the question mark?

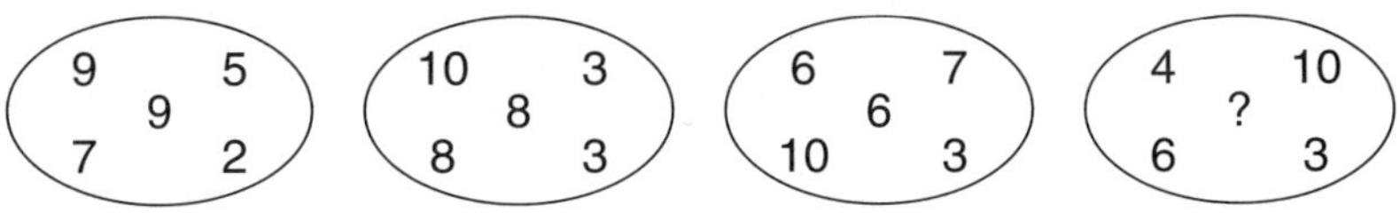

38. Which two words are opposite in meaning?

prefatory, precipitous, wholesome, riotous, sloping, fetid, noxious, exasperated

39. Which circle contains letters that will not make a word?

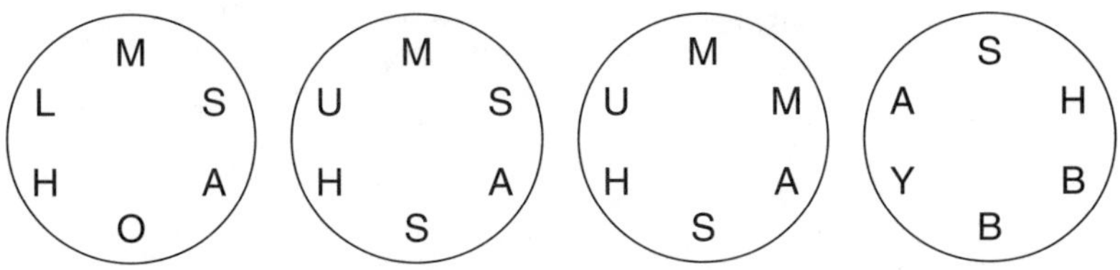

A B C D

40. Each of the nine squares in the grid marked 1A to 3C should incorporate all the lines and symbols that are shown in the squares of the same letter and number immediately above and to the left. For example, 1C should incorporate all the lines and symbols that are in 1 and C.

One of the squares is incorrect. Which one is it?

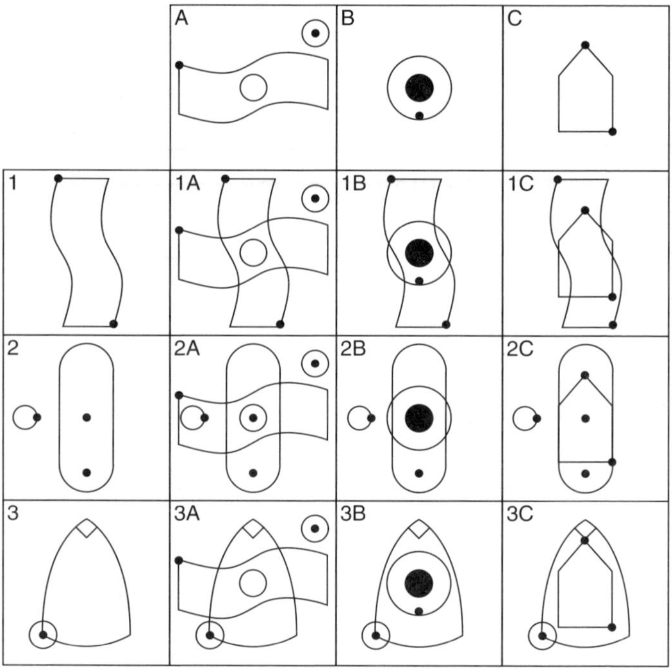

Test One: Answers

1. E: divide into groups of four identical arrows. In each group of four, each arrow moves 90 degrees clockwise. One arrow appears black in each group moving forward one place each time.

2. INSULT PRAISE

3. COSMOPOLITAN

4. 41 minutes

5. F: the figure at the top of the main figure flips into it, and the figure originally inside flips out.

6. lupine: it is a word meaning wolf-like. The remaining words are all connected with foxes.

7. FLEET

8.

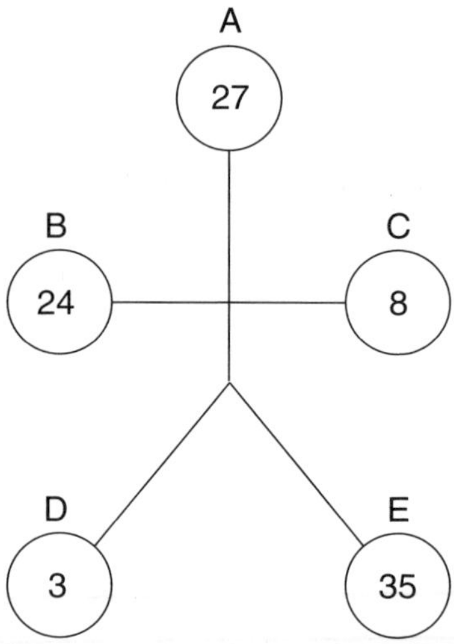

D × C = B

B + D = A

B + C + D = E

9. C: looking down, a vertical line is added to the bell, and looking across, two horizontal lines are added.

10. colour: Beaufort is a scale of wind, Munsell is a scale of colours.

11. bawdiness (wise bands)

12. d. 87923

A	B	C	D	E		B	E	D	C	A
6	4	5	2	1		4	1	2	5	6

A	B	C	D	E		B	E	D	C	A
3	8	2	9	7		8	7	9	2	3

13. 15

14. GRACIOUS MERCIFUL

15. CHINA

16. 239: $1 \times 2 + 1 = 3$; $3 \times 3 + 2 = 11$; $11 \times 4 + 3 = 47$; $47 \times 5 + 4 = 239$

17. C: each segment is a mirror image of the segment opposite, but with black/white reversal.

18. to hot up

19. 72.5: the amount deducted increases by 2.75 each time ie, 2.75, 5.5, 8.25, 11.

20. F: all the others have an identical pairing.

21. YOU CANNOT TELL HOW DEEP A PUDDLE IS UNTIL YOU STEP IN IT

22. C: the black spike moves one place clockwise, then two places, then three, then four.

23. 21

24. CHROMIUM

25. SWEEP

26. CLUTCH

27. b. an Arctic breed of dog

28. DAYDREAMER

29. F: looking both across and down, only lines or dots that are common to the first two squares are carried forward to the third square.

30. BRIGANTINE

31. d. narcotic

32. HARPSICHORD

33. LIMPET

34. A: the figure at the bottom rotates 90 degrees and goes to the left. The figure at the top rotates 180 degrees and goes inside the figure now on the left. The figure in the middle rotates 90 degrees and goes to the right.

35. 13: (5 × 8 = 40) – (3 × 9 = 27) = 13

36. STAR

37. 11: (4 + 10 = 14) – (6 – 3 = 3) = 11

38. noxious, wholesome

39. C: (A= SHALOM; B = SHAMUS; D = SHABBY)

40. 2B

Test Two: Questions

1. Which of the following is not a colour or colour shade?

   such tent   cap riot   red navel   cats lie   for fans

2. 

   What comes next?

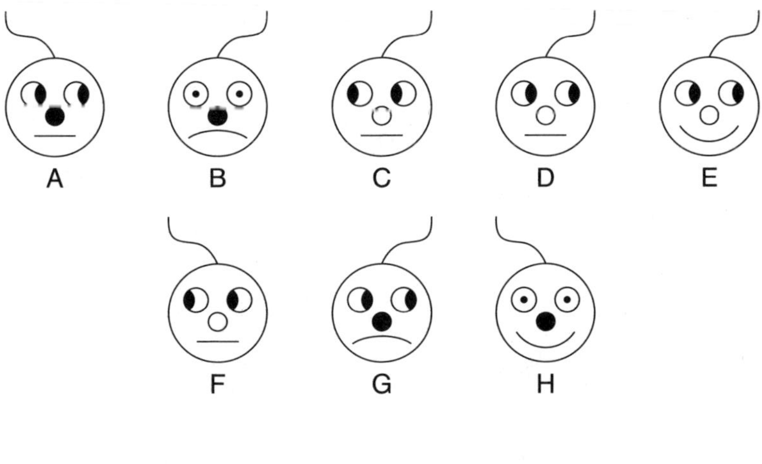

3. Find a magic number square in the grid where all lines, ie, horizontal, vertical and corner to corner, add up to the same total.

25	21	19	20	35	45
22	20	24	5	10	30
18	23	26	40	25	15
7	15	25	9	13	11
8	17	10	15	10	14
16	12	14	16	12	17
3	13	18	11	9	8

4. Which is the odd one out?

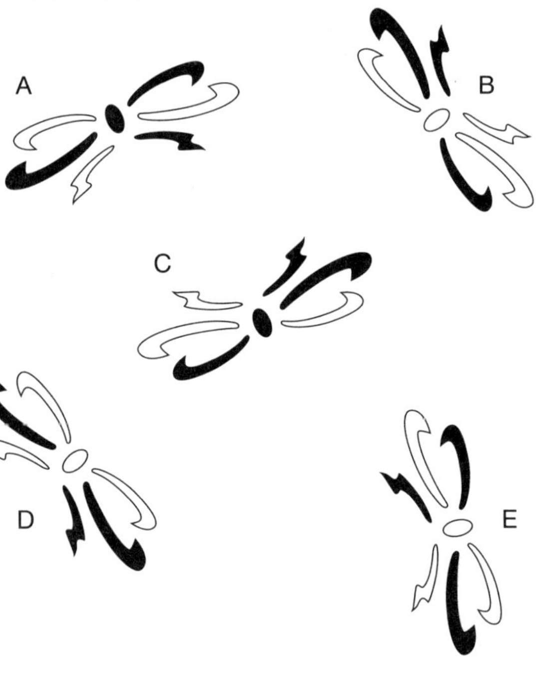

5. Which is the odd one out?

   frisk, gambol, frolic, romp, lope

6. Complete the words so that the last two letters of the first word are the first two letters of the second word etc. The last two letters of the fourth word must also be the first two letters of the first word to complete the circle.

   CO   **SS**   **AP**   **RI**

7. A train travelling at a speed of 50 mph enters a tunnel that is 1.75 miles long. The length of the train is 3/8 miles. How long does it take for all the train to pass through the tunnel, from the moment the front enters to the moment the rear emerges?

8. How many lines appear below?

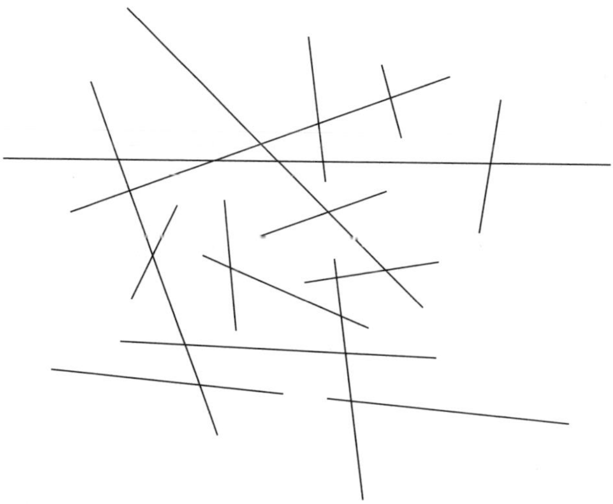

9. dormitory is to sleep as refectory is to:

   study, eat, meet, pray, speak

10. SUNDAY MONDAY TUESDAY WEDNESDAY

THURSDAY FRIDAY SATURDAY

Which day comes three days before the day that comes two days after the day that comes two days after the day that comes three days before Wednesday?

11. What numbers should replace the question marks?

3	8	2	9	1
5	7	6	4	5
8	5	8	6	7
1	9	2	8	3
5	4	6	7	5
?	?	?	?	?

12. Which is the odd one out?

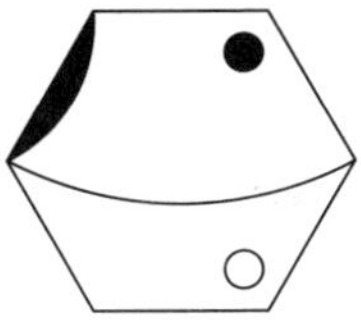

A

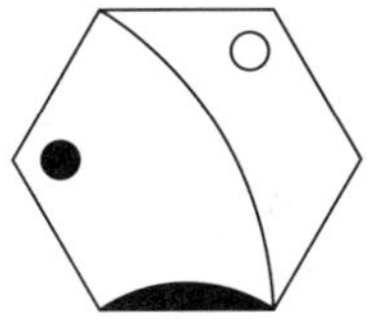

B

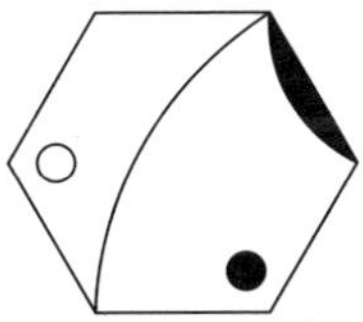

C

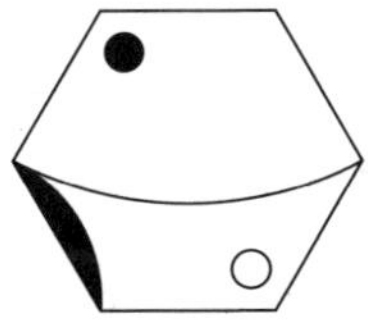

D

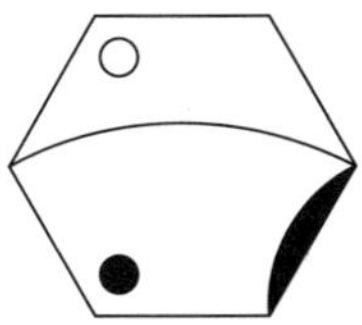

E

13. Insert the same three letters into the blank spaces to find two words that are opposite in meaning.

– – – F A N E

– – – P E R

14. Only one of the sets of five letters below can be rearranged to spell out a five-letter English word. Find the word.

JUCBI NEACH METAP TPHED MUDOP ABUMG ERVIC

15. What number should replace the question mark?

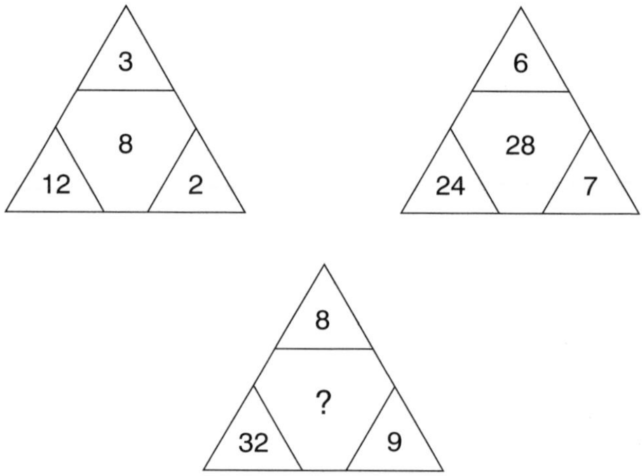

16. Which is the odd one out?

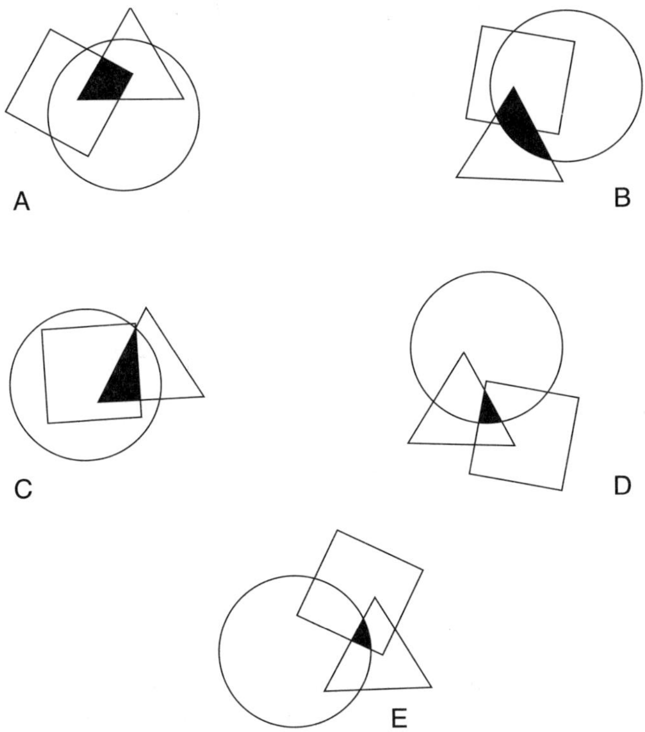

17. What is the meaning of adumbrate?

   a. come forward;

   b. to obscure;

   c. flattery;

   d. appeal to;

   e. speak off the cuff.

18. Insert the letters into the grid to form two words that together form a phrase.

    LLY COT EVA TEN MR

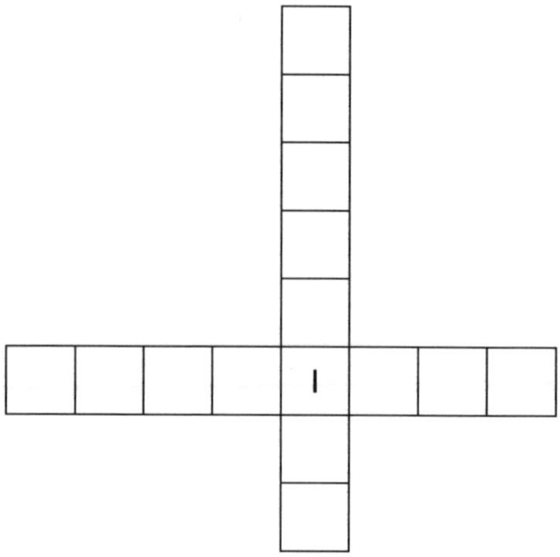

19. Insert the numbers into the circles so that, for any particular circle, the sum of the numbers in the circles connected to it equals the value corresponding to that circled number in the list.

For example:

1 = 14 (4 + 7 + 3)

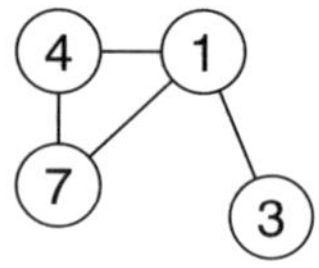

4 = 8 (7 + 1)

7 = 5 (4 + 1)

3 = 1

1 = 15

2 = 5

3 = 9

4 = 10

5 = 6

6 = 5

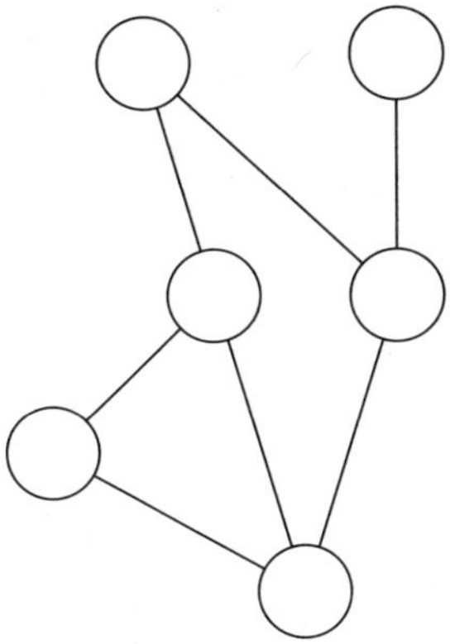

20.

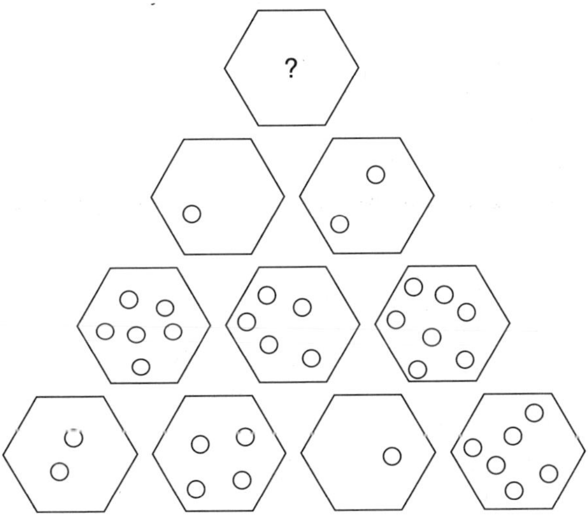

Which hexagon should replace the question mark?

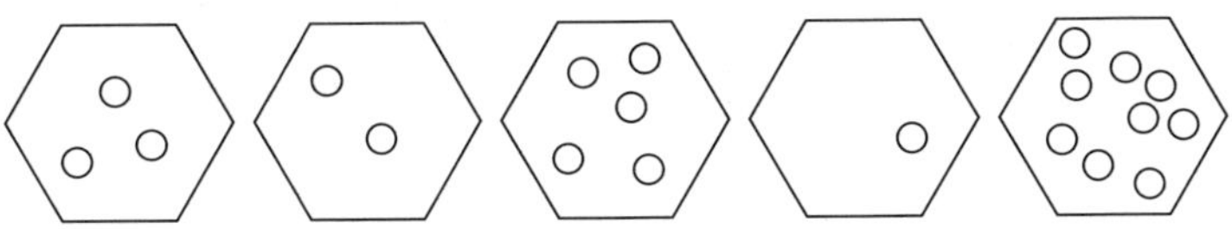

21. Place two four-letter bits together to make an eight-letter word that is a DANCE.

IHUG EARD FAMD PITE BAND

ANGO SARA HORN BUNN GALL

22.

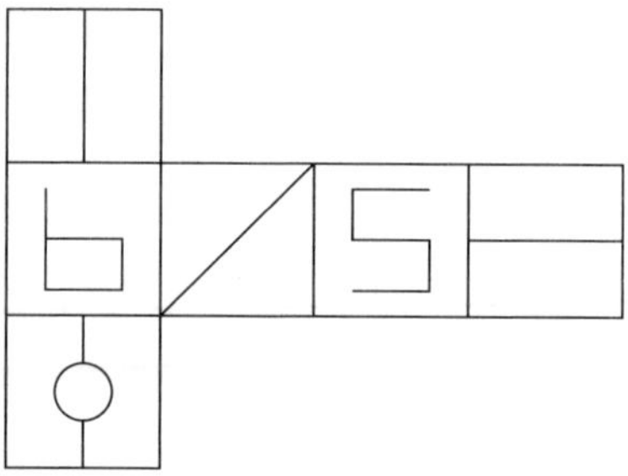

When the above is folded to form a cube, which is the only one of the following that *cannot* be produced?

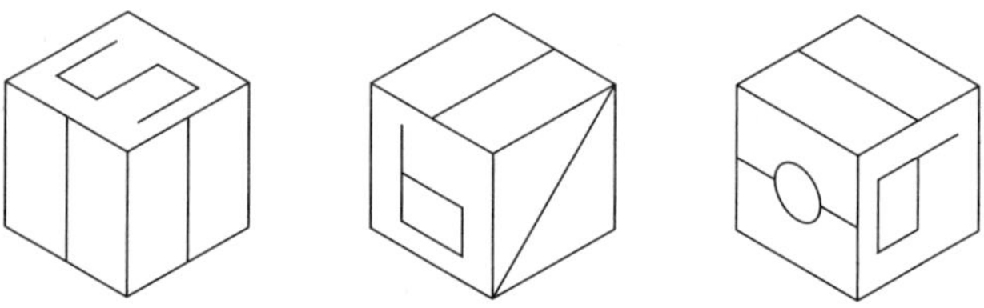

A B C

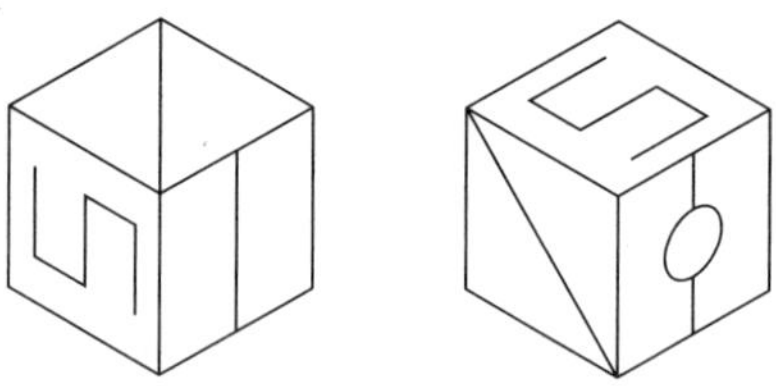

D E

23. Which is the odd one out?

a. béchamel;
b. coulomb;
c. ragout;
d. goulash;
e. gruyere.

24. Make a six-letter word out of these four letters:

R U Q E

25. Arrange the letters in the grid to form two words that are theatrical terms.

A C E E

D L M O

O R S U

26.

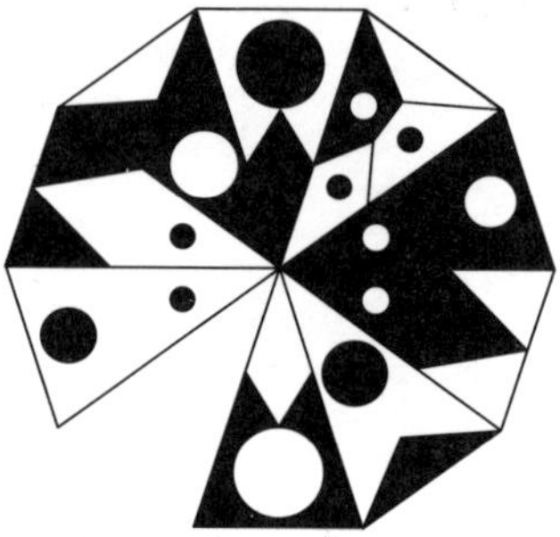

Which is the missing segment?

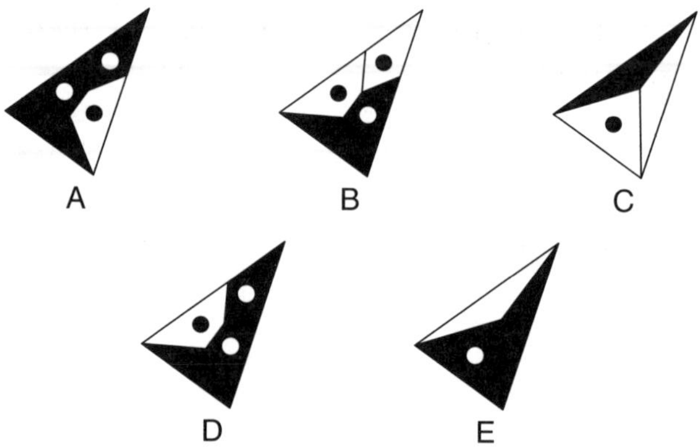

27. hedonism is to pleasure as aestheticism is to:

morality, beauty, ideas, perception, reality

28. Insert a word that completes the first word and starts the second word.

SAFETY (– – –) CUSHION

29. What is the answer to this sum in decimals?

$$\frac{7}{9} \div \frac{14}{18} \div \frac{8}{4} = x$$

30. 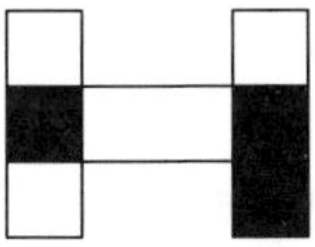 is to 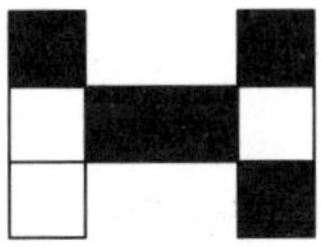

as 

is to

A B C D E

31. Change one letter in each word to make a fish.

GUNNER RIPPER WINNOW PUFFED

32. Place four two-letter bits together to equal an eight-letter word that is a vegetable (four bits are not used).

OT DA BE RO

ET SO RA AT

33. Insert a word in the brackets that means the same as the words outside the brackets.

FRESHWATER FISH (– – – –) FIND FAULT WITH

34. Which two words are similar?

INDISCRETE, DUPERY, ABERRATION, ARTIFICE, INEXPLICABLE, GUILELESS

35. Trace a temperature description. A dot separates the two words. One letter is missing.

?	A	D	E
E	R	E	L
N	G	•	A
T	I	S	C

36. Insert a word that completes the first word and starts the second word.

CHEQUERED (– – – –) POLE

37. What number should replace the question mark?

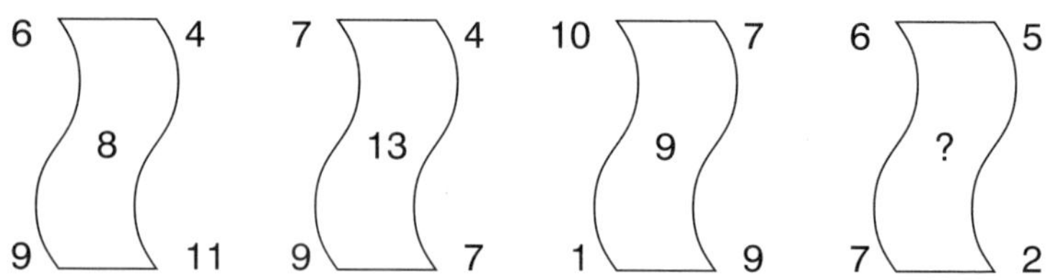

38. Find four sets of four numbers that each total 300.

27	41	67	12
89	24	168	76
6	31	123	186
154	91	75	30

39. Fill in the blanks to find two words that are synonyms (clockwise or anticlockwise).

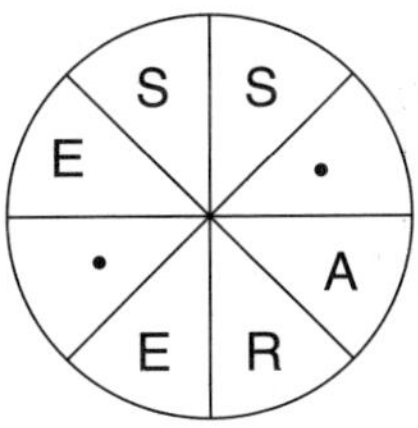

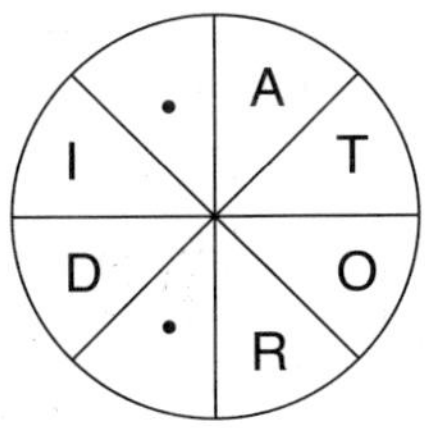

40. Each of the nine squares in the grid marked 1A to 3C should incorporate all the lines and symbols that are shown in the squares of the same letter and number immediately above and to the left. For example, 2B should incorporate all the lines and symbols that are in 2 and B.

One of the squares is incorrect. Which one is it?

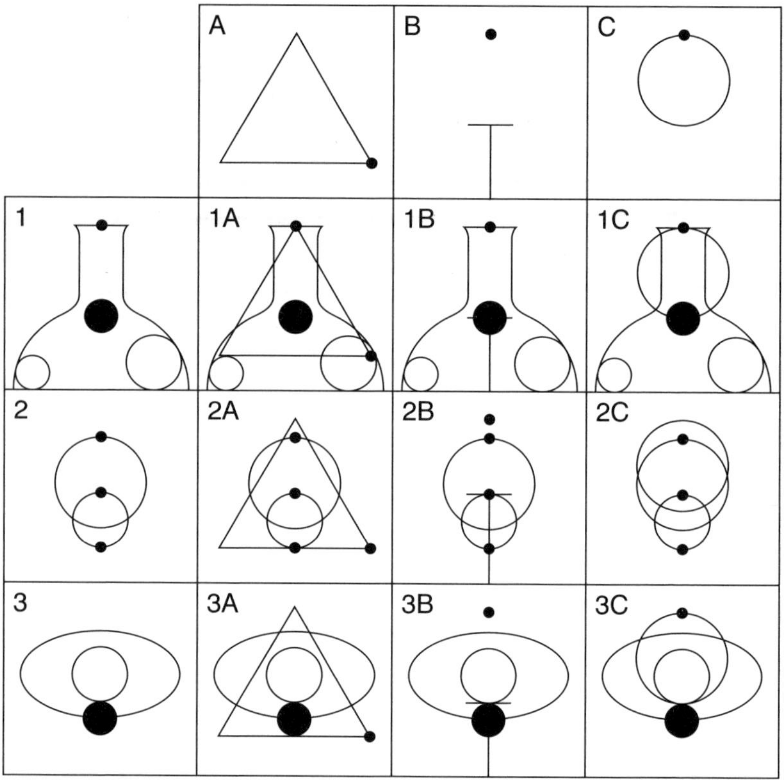

Test Two: Answers

1. cats lie = elastic. The colours are

   such tent = chestnut, cap riot = apricot,
   red navel = lavender, for fans = saffron

2. D: the curl alternates left/right, the eyes alternate left/forward/right, the nose alternates black/white and the mouth alternates happy/sad/straight.

3. 17 10 15

   12 14 16

   13 18 11

   Magic number 42

4. D: A is the same as E but with black/white reversal, and similarly B is the same as C.

5. lope

6. ALCOVE VESSEL ELAPSE SERIAL

7. 2 minutes 33 seconds (2.55 minutes). At 50 mph the train takes $2.125 \times 60 \div 50$ to pass through the tunnel, ie, 2.55 minutes.

8. 16

9. eat

10. MONDAY

11. 7 6 8 5 8. The first three lines are repeated, but reversed.

12. D: the rest are the same figure rotated.

13. PRO: PROFANE PROPER

14. TPHED = DEPTH

15. 36: $32 \div 8 \times 9 = 36$.

    Similarly $12 \div 3 \times 2 = 8$ and $24 \div 6 \times 7 = 28$

16. B: in all the others, only the portion common to all three figures is shaded.

17. b. to obscure

18. TERMINAL VELOCITY

19.

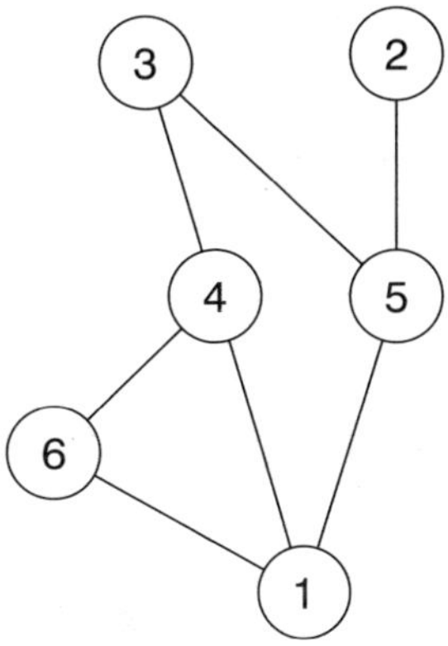

20. A: the contents of each hexagon are determined by the contents of the two hexagons directly below it. In the second row from the bottom, add the number of circles in the hexagons below. In the third row from the bottom take the difference ie, subtract, therefore, in the top circle add again, so one circle plus two circles means three circles in the top hexagon.

21. SARABAND

22. D

23. b. coulomb (electrical term). The others are food terms.

24. QUEUER

25. COSTUME LEOTARD

26. D: opposite segments are a mirror image of each other, but with black/white reversal.

27. beauty

28. PIN

29. $= \frac{7}{9} \times \frac{18}{14} \times \frac{4}{8} = 0.5$

30. B: the figures are mirror-images but with black/white reversal.

31. GUNNEL KIPPER MINNOW PUFFER

32. BEETROOT

33. CARP

34. DUPERY ARTIFICE

35. CENTIGRADE SCALE

36. FLAG

37. 16: 6 + 5 + 7 – 2 = 16

38. 186 67 6 41; 75 27 168 30; 154 24 31 91; 12 76 89 123

39. CARELESS DILATORY

40. 2C

Test Three: Questions

1.

What comes next?

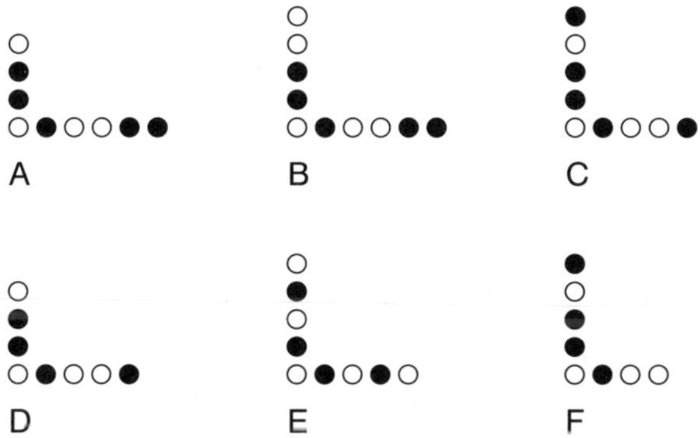

2. MEAN ACTORS is an anagram of which two words that are similar in meaning?

3. Start at one of the corner squares and spiral clockwise around the perimeter to spell out a nine-letter word, finishing at the centre square. You have to provide the missing letters.

A	S	S
*	T	T
*	A	E

4. A man jogs at 6 mph over a certain journey and walks back over the same journey at 3 mph. What is his average speed for the journey?

5.

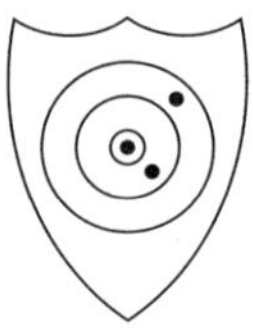

The contents of which shield below are most like the contents of the shield above?

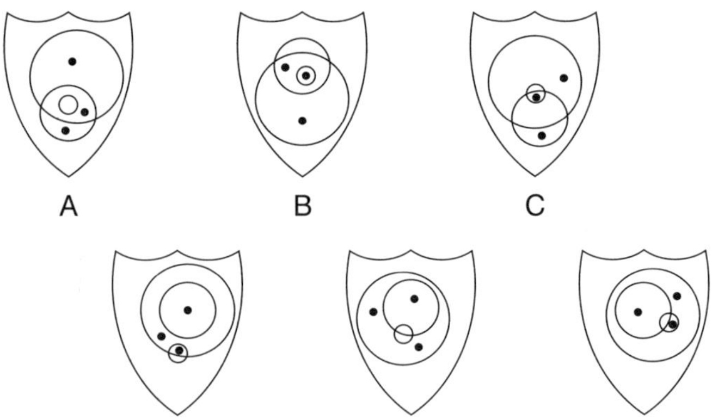

6. Which word can be placed in the brackets that has the same meaning as the definitions either side of the brackets?

IMPEDE (− − − − − −) LARGE BASKET

7. If a car had increased its average speed for a 210-mile journey by 5 mph, the journey would have been completed in one hour less. What was the original speed of the car for the journey?

8.

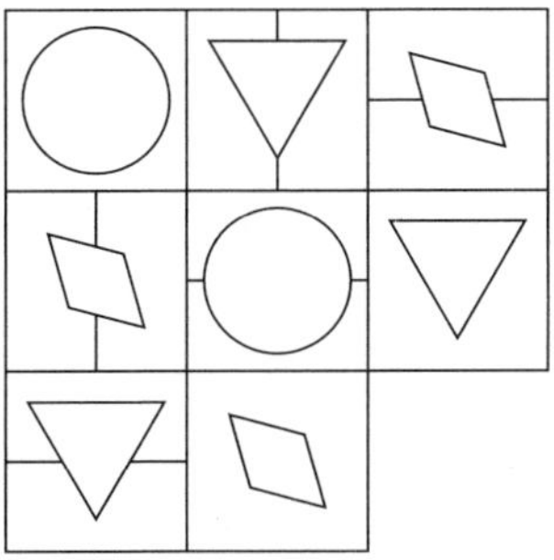

Which is the missing square?

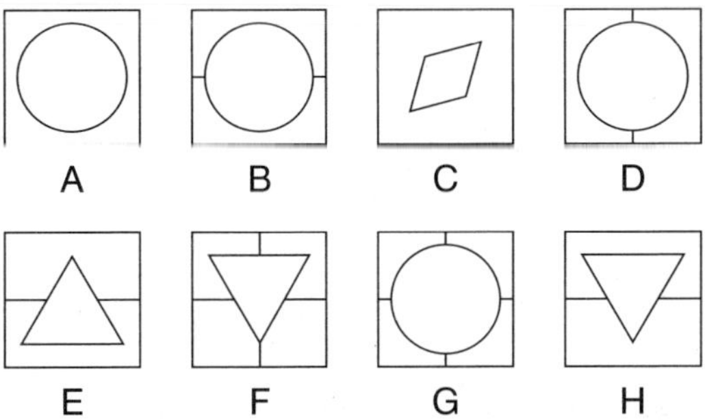

9. Which is the odd one out?

mollify, mitigate, indurate, macerate, temper

10. Solve the cryptic clue. The answer is a 13-letter word anagram within the clue:

    reword a keen phrase as in classic theatrical tradition

11. Which word below is in the wrong column?

sinistral	recto
southpaw	dextral
larboard	verso
	starboard

12. What number should replace the question mark?

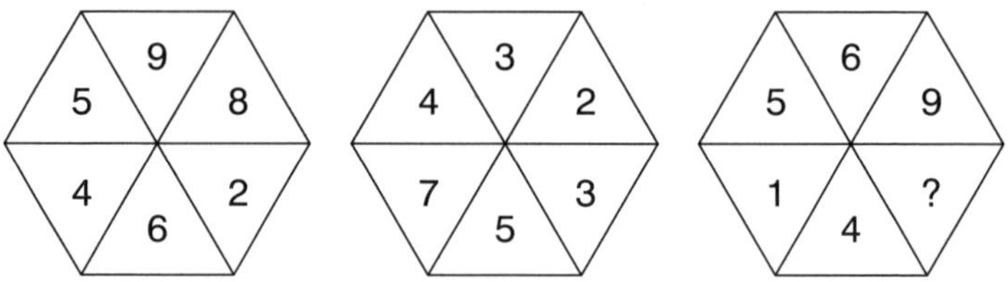

13. 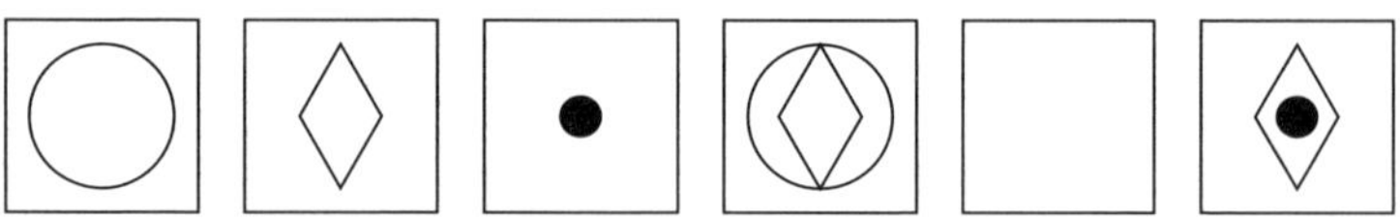

What comes next?

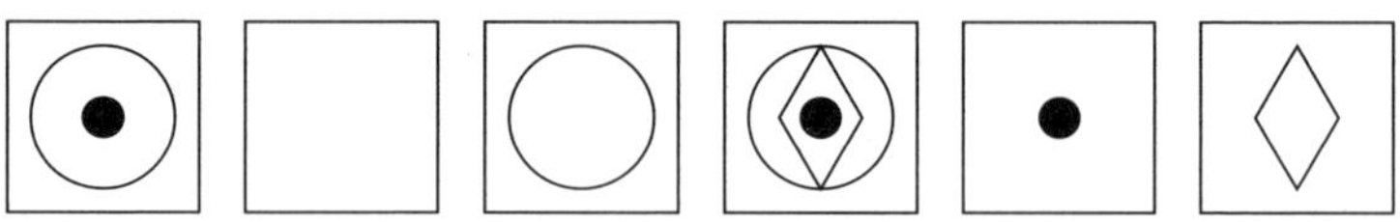

A B C D E F

14. passé is to outmoded as obsolete is to:
    stale, superseded, antediluvian, vintage, timeworn

15. Find the starting point and work from letter to letter horizontally, vertically or diagonally to spell out a 17-letter phrase.

E	S	N		
K	L	O		
I	R	I	K	E
		E	L	F
		H	T	A

16. At 12 noon my watch was correct. However, it then started to lose 18 minutes per hour. Four hours ago it stopped completely and is now showing the time as 15.30. What is the correct time?

17. 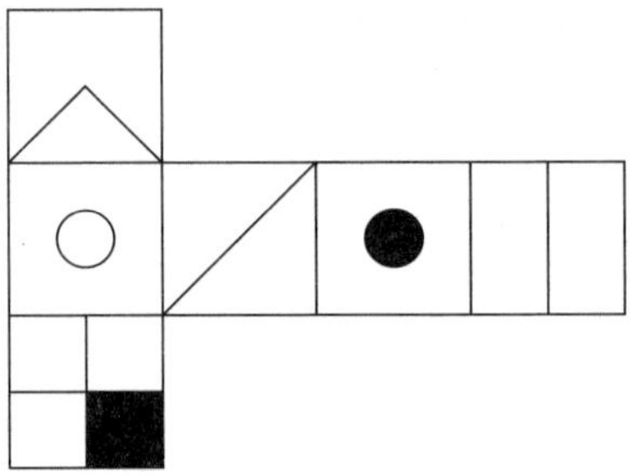

When the above is folded to form a cube, which one of the following can be produced?

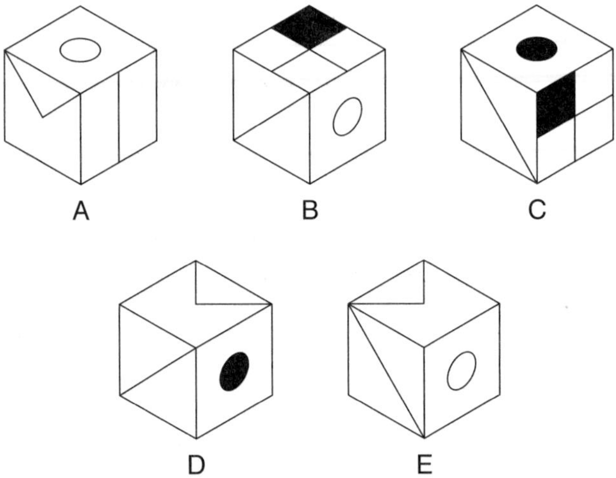

18. Which of the following is not an anagram of a type of building?

spoil hat   my bases   pet hens   eel clog   admit us

19. What continues the following sequence?

1, 2.65, 4.3, 5.95, 7.6, ?

20.

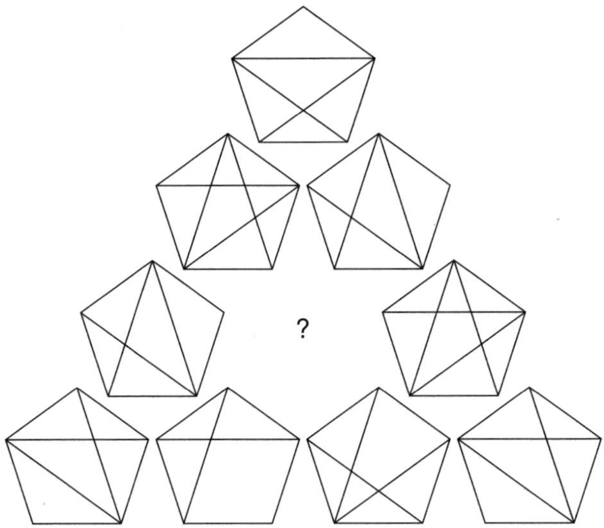

Which is the missing pentagon?

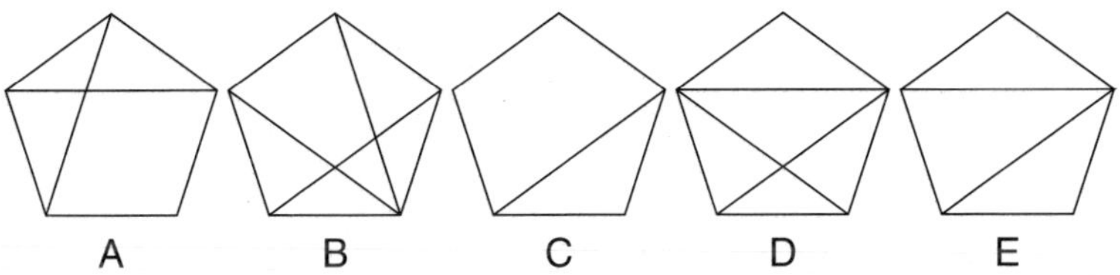

21. All the vowels have been omitted from this trite saying, see if you can replace them.

DNTBL VNSPR STTNT BRNGS BDLCK

22.

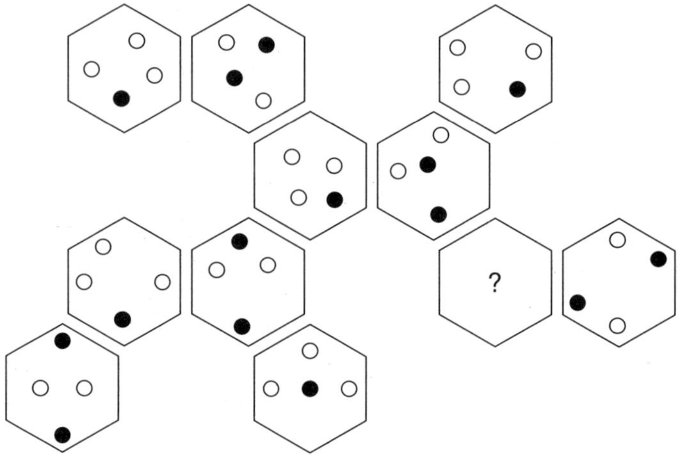

Which hexagon should replace the question mark?

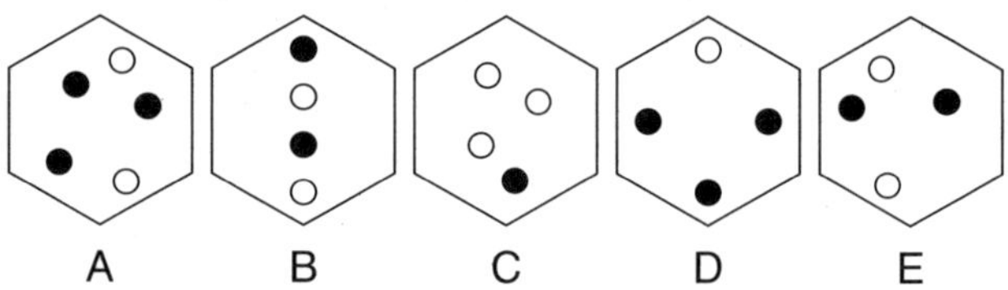

23. What is a PLECTRUM?

a. a spike of ivory;

b. part of the kidney;

c. a pick me up;

d. a flower;

e. a raised platform.

24. What is the meaning of LACINIATED?

    a. HONEYCOMBED;

    b. JAGGED;

    c. SMOOTH;

    d. STICKY;

    e. TEARFUL.

25. Which word means the same as CALUMNY?

    a. IGNOMINY;

    b. PAROXYSM;

    c. EDICT;

    d. INSURRECTION.

26. Place two three-letter bits together to equal a six-letter word that is a BUILDING TERM.

    OVE ANN ATR

    IEM ALO EXE

27. Which is the odd one out?

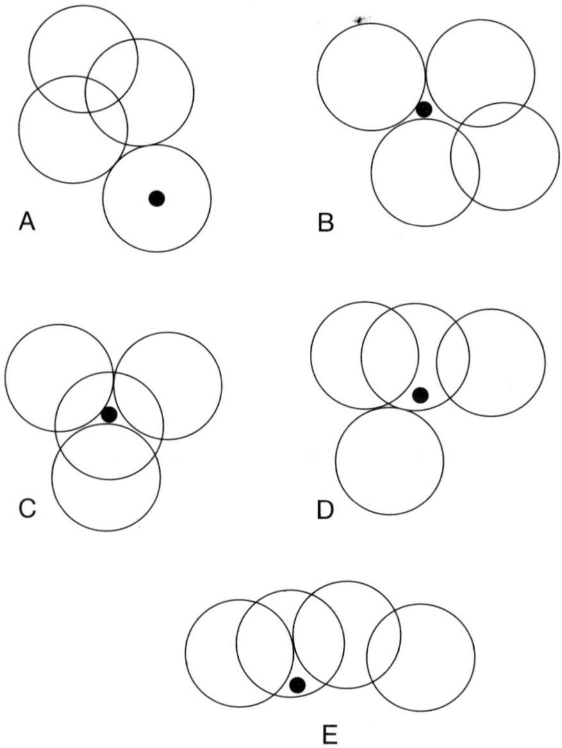

28. Which circle does not contain letters that will make a word?

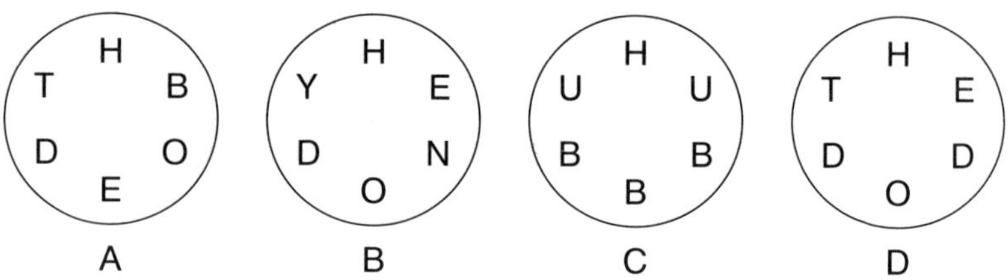

29. Fill in the blanks to find two words that are ANTONYMS (clockwise or anticlockwise)

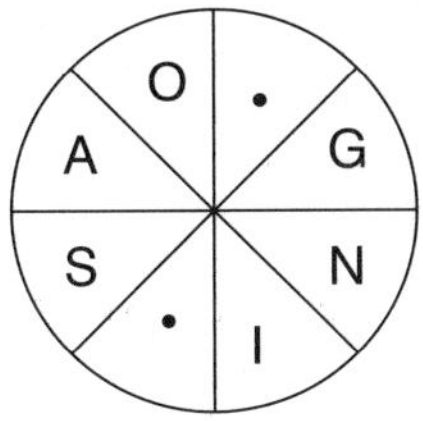

30. Letters are traced across the circle by chords. If the next letter is four letters or less away it will be found by tracing around the circumference.

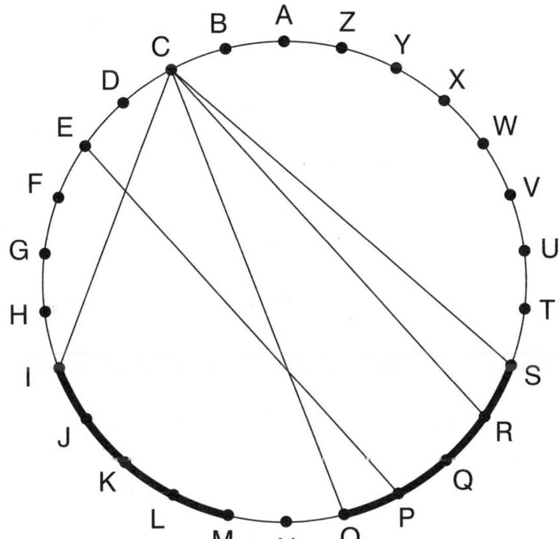

Clue: MAKES THINGS LARGER BUT IT IS SMALL (10 letters)

31. Find four sets of four numbers each set totalling 100.

20	33	16	5
24	20	29	18
15	40	11	19
4	41	34	71

32. Place a word within the brackets that means the same as the two words outside the brackets.

ECCENTRIC PERSON (– – – – –) START AN OLD CAR

33. Insert a word that completes the first word and starts the second word.

ROOMING (– – – – –) MARTIN

34. What number should replace the question mark?

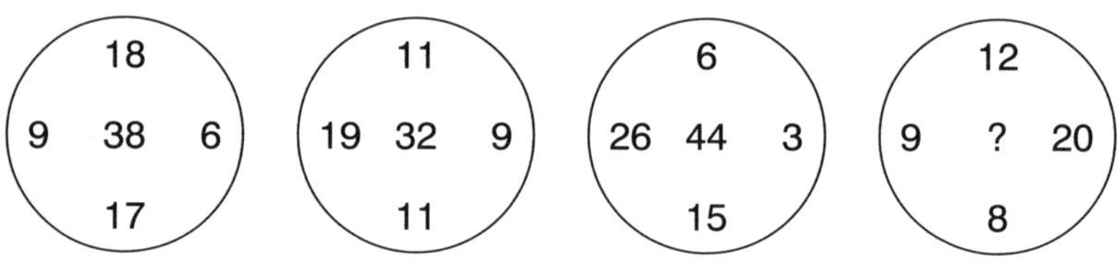

35.

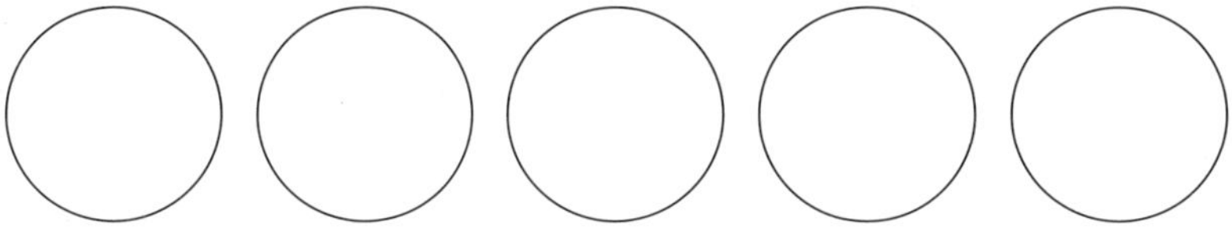

Place the number 1–5 in the circles so that:

the sum of the numbers 2 and 4 and all the numbers between them total 15;

the sum of the numbers 3 and 2 and all the numbers between them total 11;

the sum of the numbers 5 and 4 and all the numbers between them total 12;

the sum of the numbers 1 and 3 and all the numbers between them total 9.

36. What number should replace the question mark?

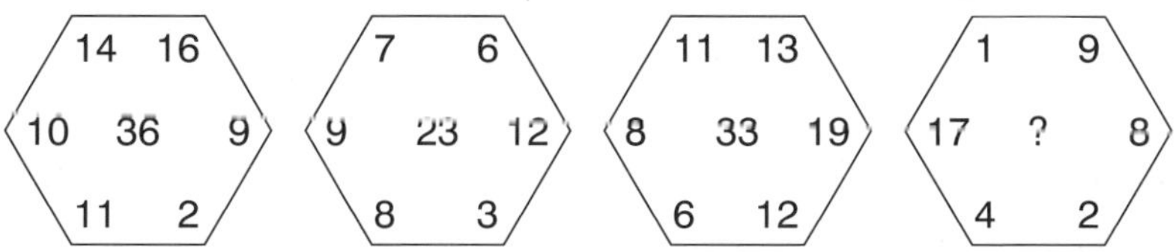

37. Which of these is not an anagram of a FLOWER?

a. AALAZE; b. SSOOCM; c. TTRUBO;

d. HADAIL; e. LLOMAW.

38.

To which pentagon below can a dot be added so that it meets the same conditions as in the pentagon above?

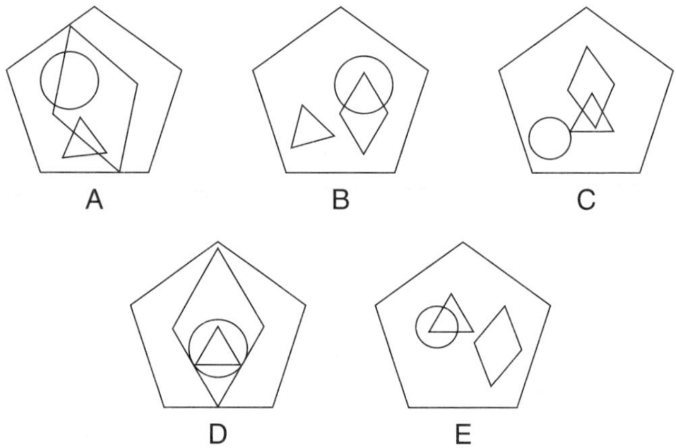

39. Which word means the same as GIMCRACK?

a. LUCID;

b. CHIMERA;

c. CONVEX;

d. BAUBLE.

40. Each of the nine squares in the grid marked 1A to 3C should incorporate all the lines and symbols that are shown in the squares of the same letter and number immediately above and to the left. For example, 2B should incorporate all the lines and symbols that are in 2 and B.

One of the squares is incorrect. Which one is it?

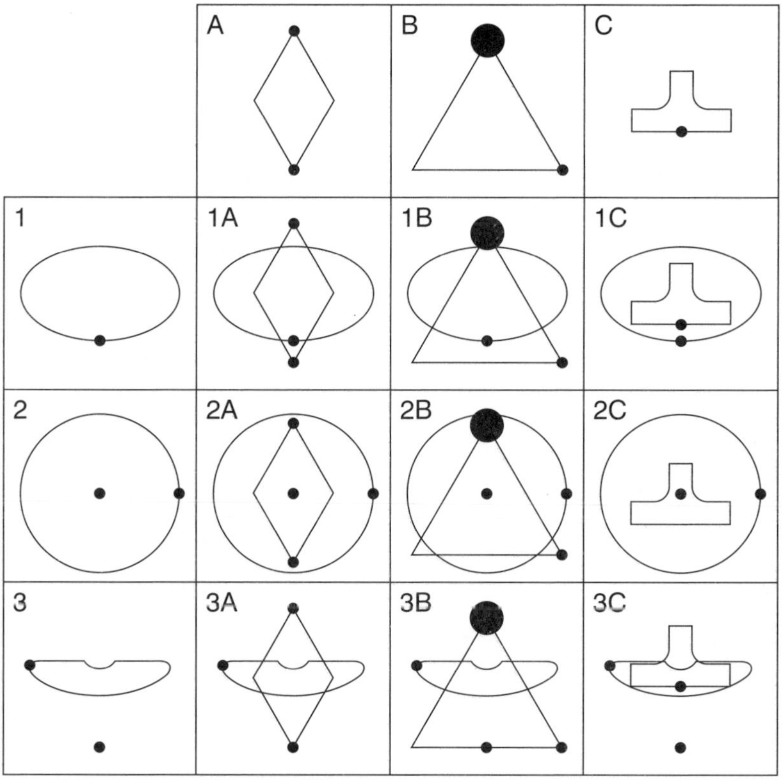

Test Three: Answers

1. D: first add one black dot to the horizontal, then two black dots to the vertical, then one white dot to the vertical and then two white dots to the horizontal.

2. SCENT AROMA

3. STEADFAST

4. 4 mph. Say the journey is six miles each way. Then at 6 mph the outward jog would take one hour and the inward walk two hours. This means he takes three hours to travel 12 miles or one hour to travel four miles.

5. B: it contains one dot in one circle, one dot in two circles and one dot in three circles.

6. HAMPER

7. 30 mph

8. D: each horizontal and vertical line contains a circle, triangle and diamond, also one square has no line, one has a vertical line and one a horizontal line.

9. indurate: this is a word meaning harden, the other words mean soften.

10. Shakespearean (a keen phrase as)

11. verso, which is a word meaning a left-hand page and should, therefore, be in the left-hand column.

12. 5: the difference between 6 and 1 is 5, and the difference between 9 and 4 is 5. Similarly the difference between 7 and 3 is 4 and the difference between 5 and 2 is 3.

13. C: each fourth square contains a circle, each alternate square contains a diamond and each third square contains a dot.

14. superseded

15. LIKE FATHER LIKE SON

16. 9 pm

17. C

18. pet hens = Stephen. The buildings are:
spoil hat = hospital, my bases = embassy,
eel clog = college and admit us = stadium.

19. 9.25: add 1.65 each time.

20. D: the contents of each pentagon are determined by the contents of the two pentagons immediately below it. Lines are carried forward from these two pentagons, except when two lines appear in the same position, in which case they are cancelled out.

21. DON'T BELIEVE IN SUPERSTITION IT BRINGS BAD LUCK

22. C: so that each adjoining pair of hexagons contains three black dots and five white dots.

23. a. a spike of ivory

24. b. JAGGED

25. a. IGNOMINY

26. ANNEXE

27. B: in all the others the dot is in just one circle. In B it isn't in any of the circles.

28. D: (A = HOTBED; B = HOYDEN; C = HUBBUB)

29. HUMILITY   BOASTING

30. MICROSCOPE

31. 24 19 41 16;   71 5 20 4;   18 15 34 33;   11 20 29 40

32. CRANK

33. HOUSE

34. 9: 12 + 9 + 8 – 20 = 9

35. 21534 or 43512. Note that the sum of the numbers 1–5 is 15. According to the first line of the question, the numbers 2 and 4 must, therefore, be in the outside circles.

36. 29: 17 + 1 + 9 + 8 – (4 + 2)

37. c. TURBOT (fish): a. AZALEA; b. COSMOS; d. DAHLIA; e. MALLOW

38. E: so that the dot can be placed in the circle and the triangle only.

39. BAUBLE

40. 2C

Test Four: Questions

1.

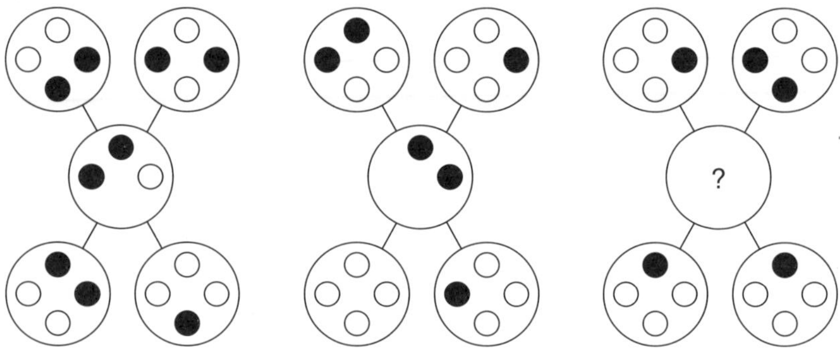

Which circle should replace the question mark?

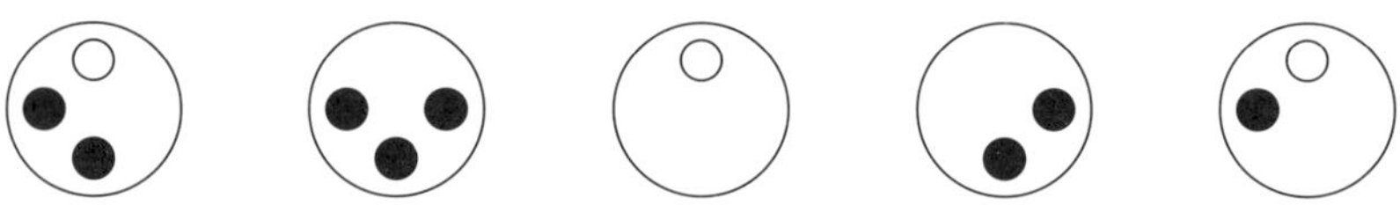

A B C D E

2. Which of these two words are most opposite in meaning?

   wizened, witless, plump, lavish, taciturn, feasible

3. Solve the cryptic clue. The answer is a 13-letter word anagram within the clue:

   redraw tennis cartoon with trepidation

4. What number should replace the question mark?

42	15	14
56	35	8
36	?	4

5. 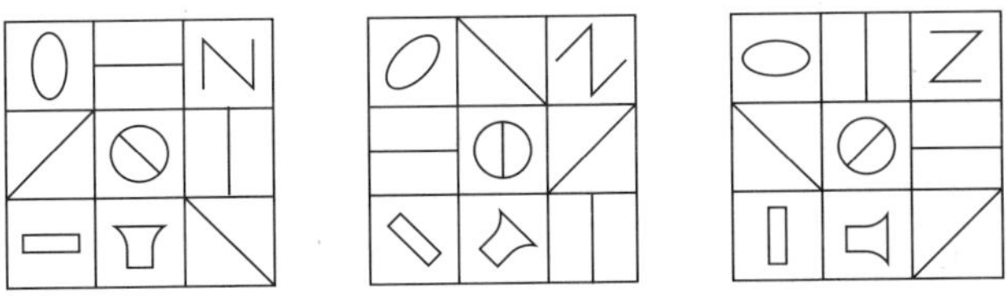

What comes next?

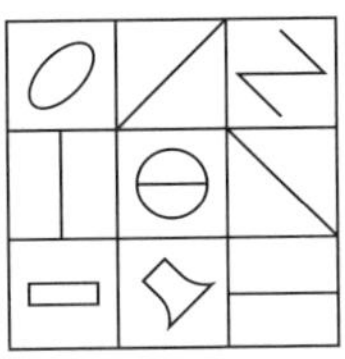

A

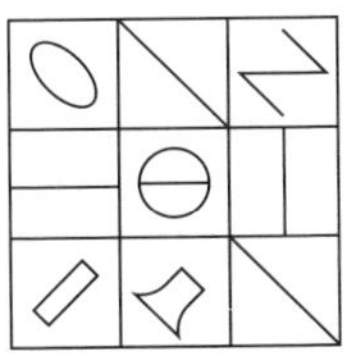

B

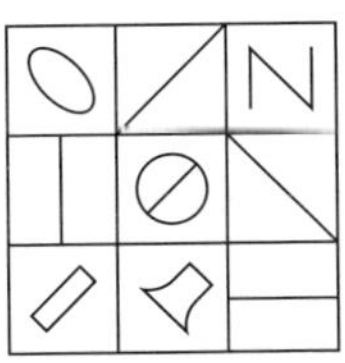

C

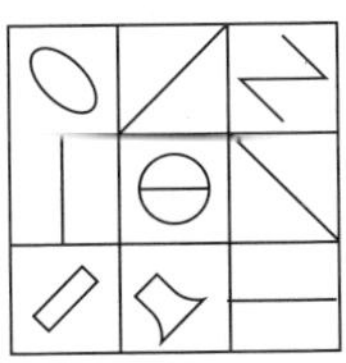

D

6. Which word in brackets is closest in meaning to the word in capitals?

FINESSE (cessation, cleverness, showiness, excellence, opening)

7. Find a word that when tacked onto the end of the first word produces another word or phrase and when placed in front of the second word produces another word or phrase.

FREE (– – – –) APART

8. 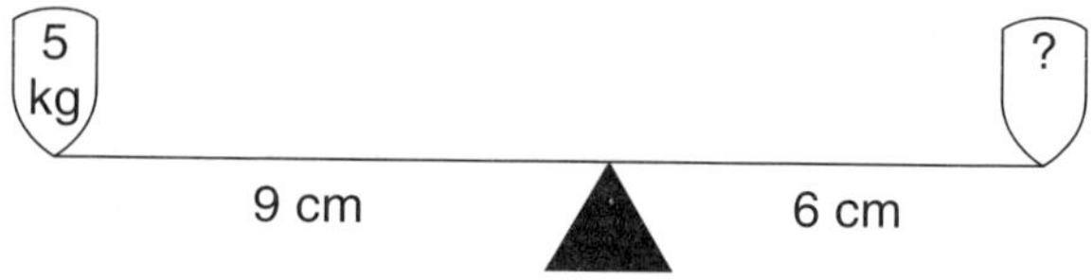

What value of weight should be placed on the scales to balance?

9. Which is the odd one out?

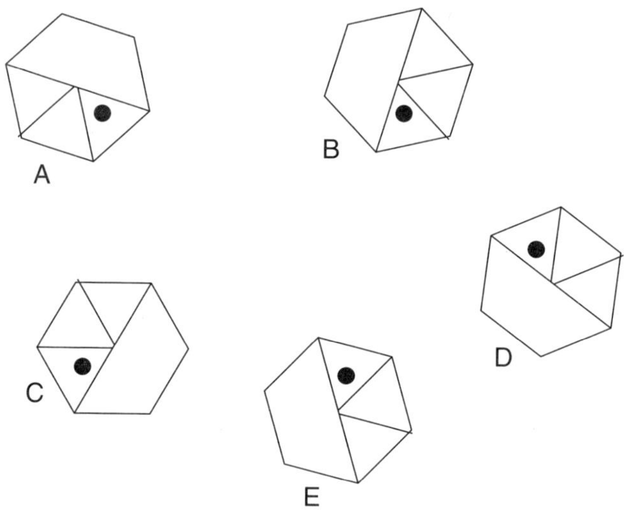

10. Change one letter only in each word to produce a familiar phrase:

    dear if bear put

11. What number should replace the question mark?

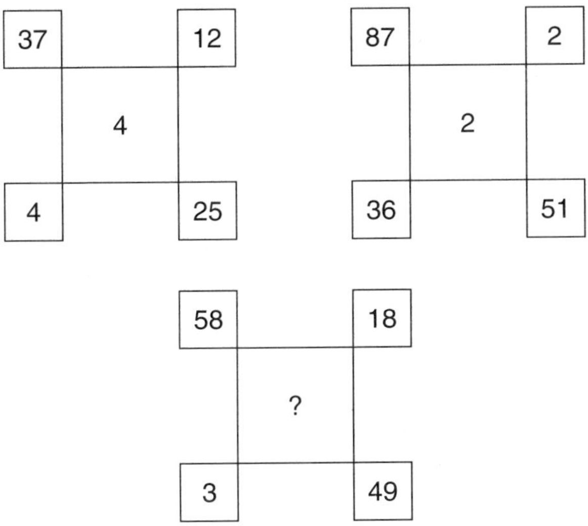

12. 

is to 

as

is to

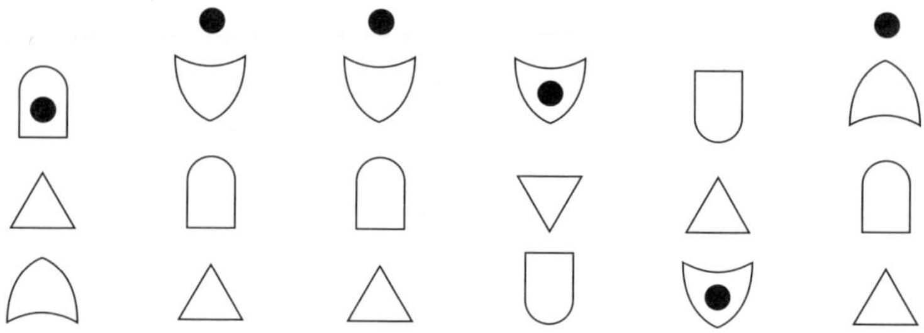

A B C D E F

13. Which is the odd one out?

fedora, sabot, tarboosh, biretta, cloche

14. Place a three-letter word in the brackets that has the same meaning as the definitions either side of the brackets.

a demand for payment (– – –) a brownish-grey colour

15. What number should replace the question mark?

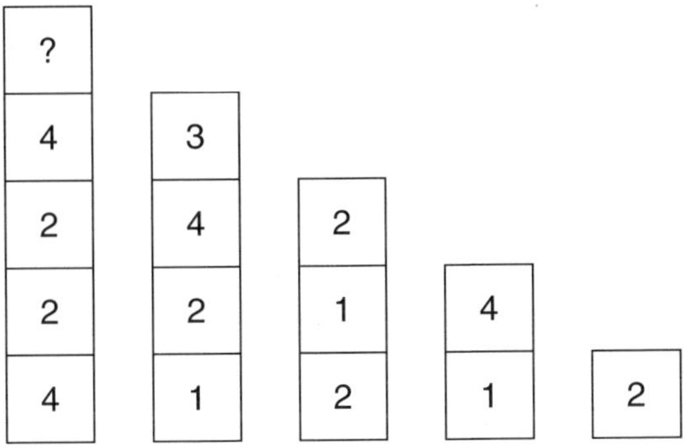

16. Which is the odd one out?

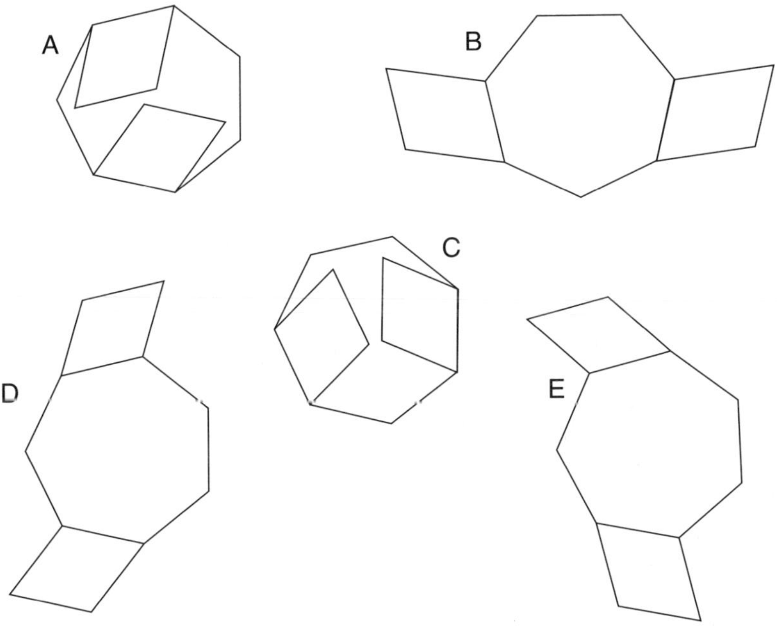

17. palmate is to hand as auriculate is to: nose, face, ear, smell, heel

18. Work from letter to adjacent letter horizontally, vertically and diagonally to spell out a 17-letter phrase.

V	O	D		
E	E	N		
R	B	B	R	A
		A	W	D
		K	C	S

19. What number should replace the question mark?

5	7	4
8	3	6
2	0	1

2	1	2
1	7	1
4	5	6

3	2	4
1	?	3
4	5	3

20.

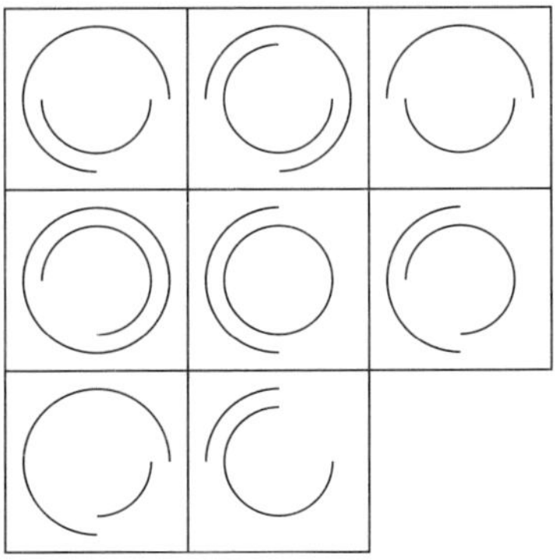

Which is the missing square?

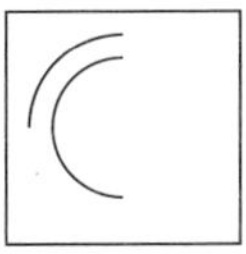
A

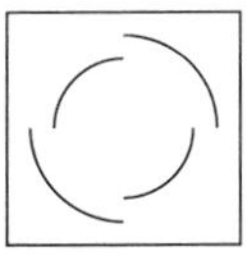
B

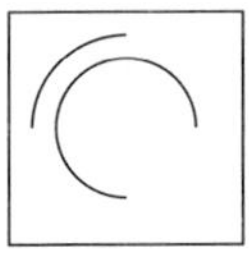
C

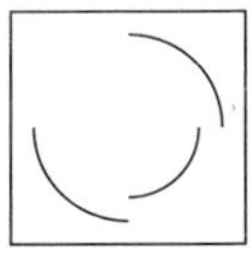
D

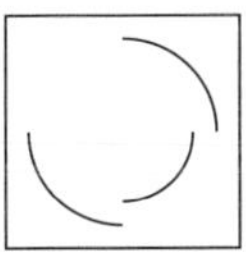
E

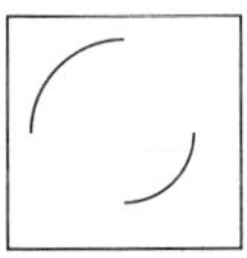
F

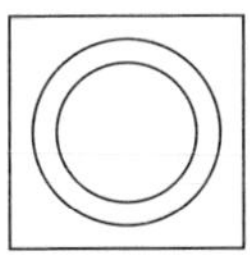
G

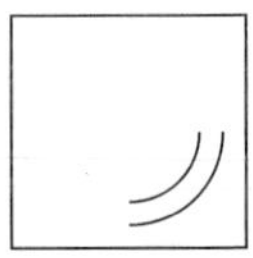
H

21. Place two four-letter bits together to make an eight-letter word that is something that can be worn.

FURB SUIT SWIN SHOU SHES SAND

BATH GALO ROBO ELOU

22. 

Which shield below is most like the shield above?

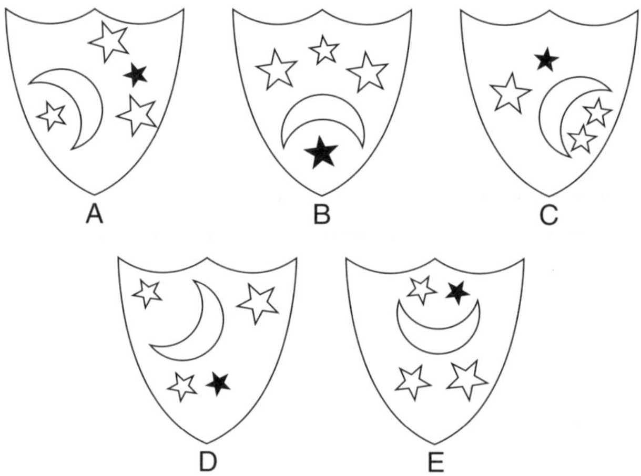

23. Find a one-word anagram for:

RAVE MICK

24. Which of these is not the anagram of a FRUIT?

a. AAANNB;

b. AAANNS;

c. RRCHYE;

d. WWPPAA;

e. PIBSEC.

25. Change one letter in each word to make a BIRD.

    STRIKE   BARBER   THOUGH   THRUST

26. Which word is the opposite of JOCUND?

    a. PELLUCID;

    b. FLACCID;

    c. SLOTHFUL;

    d. PLIABLE.

27. What word can be prefixed to these words to make new words?

    DAY   SHINE   BEAM   RISE   BONNET

28. Fill in the blanks to find a type of AIRCRAFT (clockwise or anticlockwise).

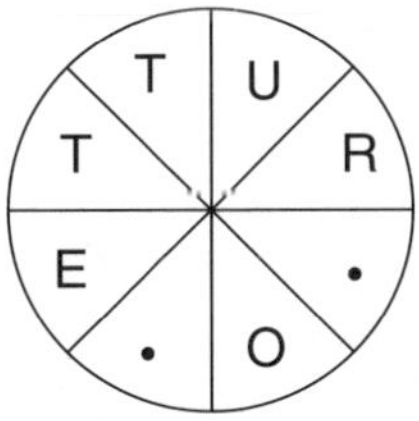

29. Visit each circle once only to spell out a 10-letter word.

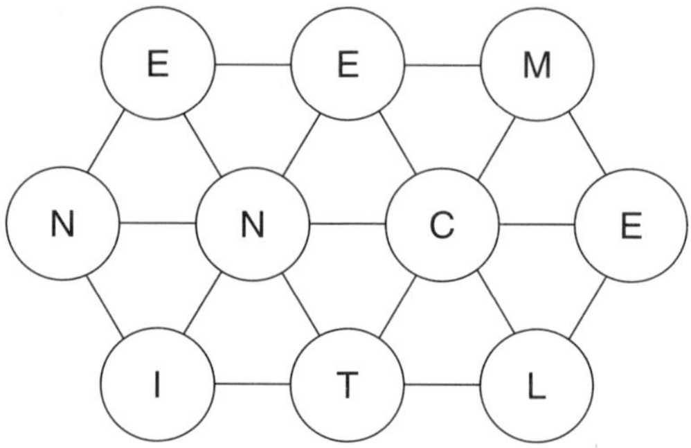

30. Letters are traced across the circle by chords. If the next letter is four letters or less away it will be found by tracing around the circumference.

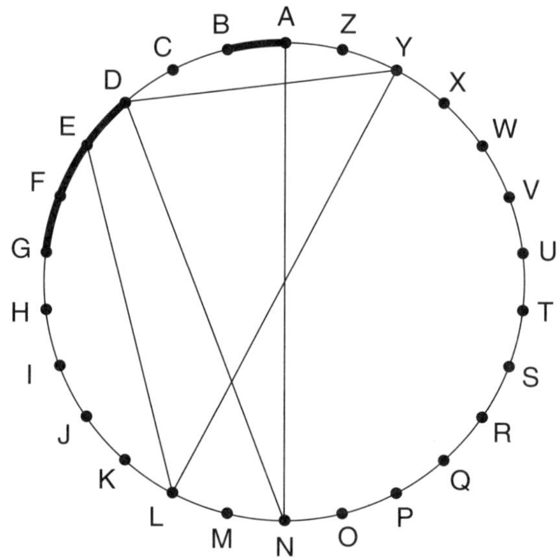

Clue: MAKE A GOOD HORSE RIDER? (two words, five and six letters)

31. Place a word inside the brackets that means the same as the two words outside the brackets.

SHEPHERD'S STAFF (– – – – –) ROGUE

32. 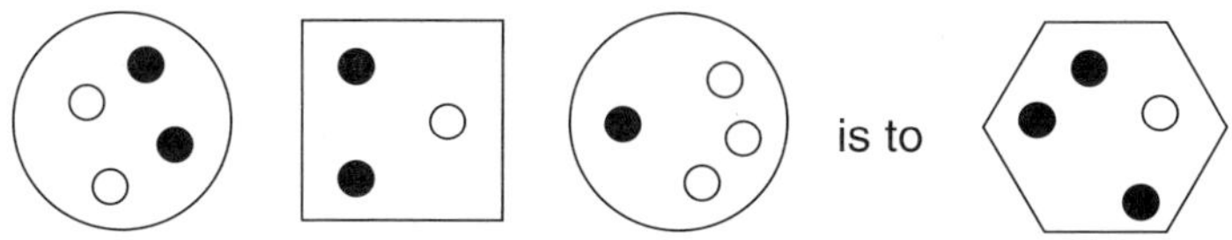

as

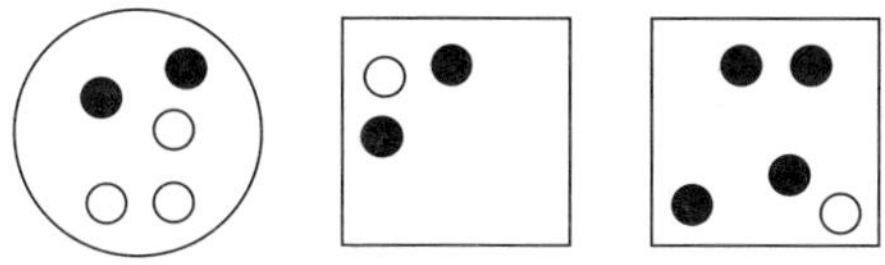

is to

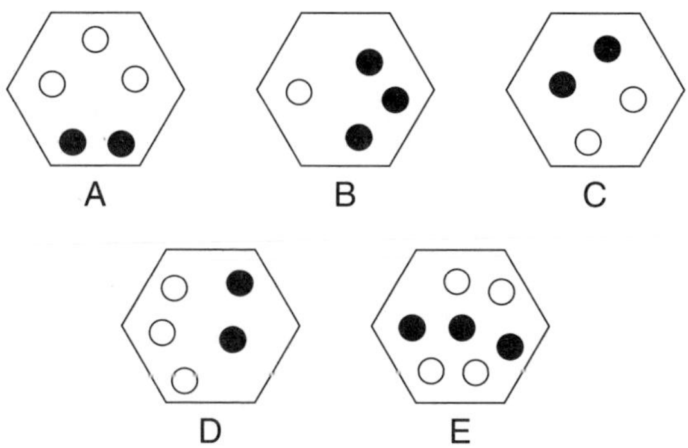

33. What does the word GORAL mean?

a. a form of epilepsy;   b. an antelope;

c. a duck from Malaysia;   d. a goshawk;

e. grain production.

34.

		A		E
	A		O	
A				
	O			E
E			E	

Insert the consonants below into the grid so that the same five five-letter words can be read both across and down.

R C C P G S N S N S P S N T T N

35. What is HIRCINE?

a. rough; b. folded;

c. sharp; d. goat-like.

36. Find the value of the question mark.

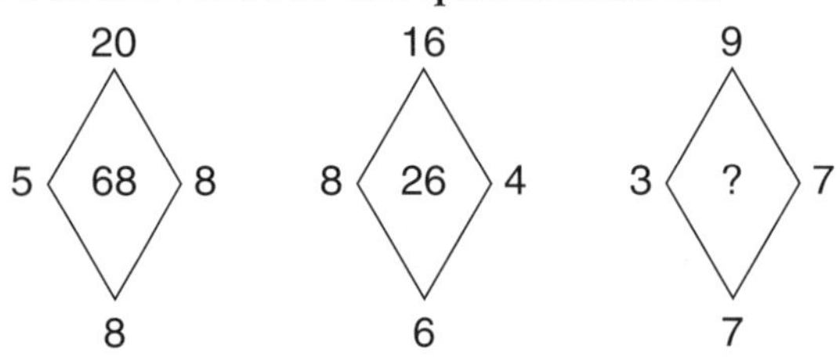

37. Fill in the blanks to find two words that are ANTONYMS (clockwise or anticlockwise).

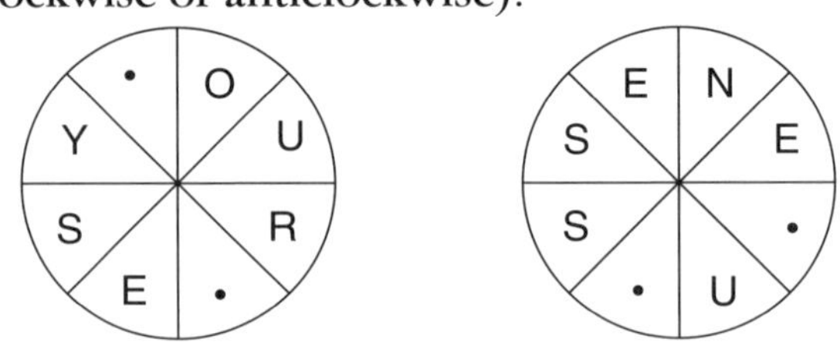

38. Insert a word that completes the first word and starts the second word.

HALF (– – – – –) BLACK

39.

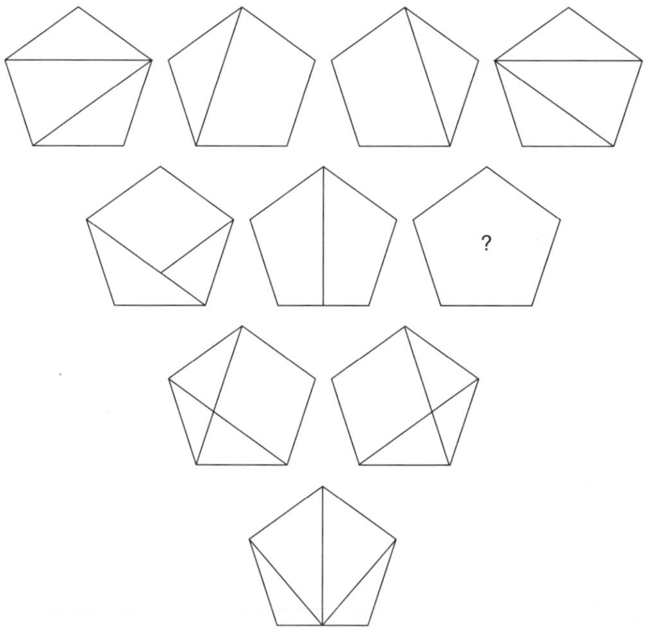

Which pentagon should replace the question mark?

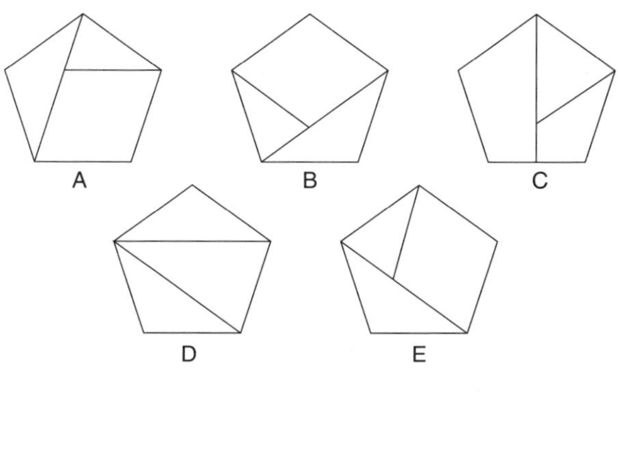

40.

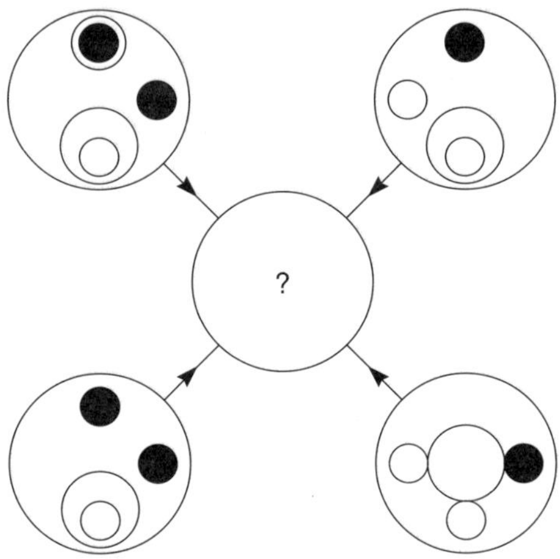

Each line and symbol that appears in the four outer circles above is transferred to the centre circle according to these rules:

If a line or symbol occurs in the outer circles:

once: it is transferred;

twice: it is possibly transferred;

three times: it is transferred;

four times: it is not transferred.

Which of the circles A, B, C, D or E shown below should appear at the centre of the diagram above?

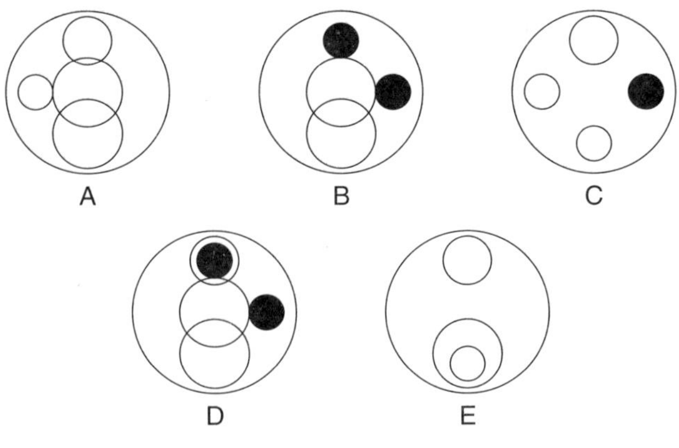

Test Four: Answers

1. B: circles are only transferred to the middle circle when they appear in the same position just once in the four surrounding circles.

2. wizened, plump

3. consternation (tennis cartoon)

4. 45: 36 ÷ 4 × 5; similarly 56 ÷ 8 × 5 = 35 and 42 ÷ 14 × 5 = 15

5. D: each segment is moving 45 degrees clockwise at each stage.

6. cleverness

7. FALL

8. 7.5 kg: 9 × 5 = 45 and 6 × 7.5 = 45

9. B: the rest are the same figure rotated.

10. year in year out

11. 6: 58 – 49 = 9   3 × 18 = 54   54 ÷ 9 = 6

12. B: the middle figure goes to the bottom, the right-hand figure goes to the top and rotates 180 degrees, the left-hand figure goes to the middle and rotates 180 degrees. The black dot goes to the top.

13. sabot: it is a shoe, the rest are hats.

14. dun

15. 6: looking at the rows of numbers across, the totals from the top are 6, 7, 8, 9, 10

16. D: A is the same as E with flaps in/out and similarly, B is the same as C.

17. ear

18. bend over backwards

19. 0: all numbers in the same position in each of the three squares add up to 10. Also, numbers formed in lines across add up to 1,110, eg, 574 + 212 + 324 = 1,110

20. F: in each horizontal and vertical row of squares, the contents of the third square are determined by the contents of the first two squares. Lines are carried forward only when they appear in the same position in the first two squares.

21. GALOSHES

22. B: the black star is by the concave side of the moon.

23. MAVERICK

24. e. BICEPS (part of body).

    a. BANANA; b. ANANAS; c. CHERRY; d. PAWPAW.

25. SHRIKE, BARBET, CHOUGH, THRUSH

26. c. SLOTHFUL

27. SUN

28. TURBOJET

29. CLEMENTINE

30. BANDY LEGGED

31. CROOK

32. C: only black dots from the circles and white dots from the squares are carried forward to the hexagon.

33. b. an antelope

34.

S	C	A	P	E
C	A	N	O	N
A	N	G	S	T
P	O	S	S	E
E	N	T	E	R

35. d. goat-like

36. 52: $20 \div 5 = 4$ $16 \div 8 = 2$ $9 \div 3 = 3$

$8 \times 8 = 64$ $4 \times 6 = 24$ $7 \times 7 = 49$

$4 + 64 = 68$ $2 + 24 = 26$ $3 + 49 = 52$

37. COURTESY RUDENESS

38. PENNY

39. B: if you draw a line down the centre to divide the set of pentagons into two halves, the right half is a mirror image of the left half.

40. D

Test Five: Questions

1. Place the letters correctly into the quadrants indicated so that two words of opposite meaning are produced, one reading round the inner circle and one round the outer circle. One word will appear clockwise and the other anti-clockwise.

NE: READ

SE: YONA

NW: BILT

SW: VOTE

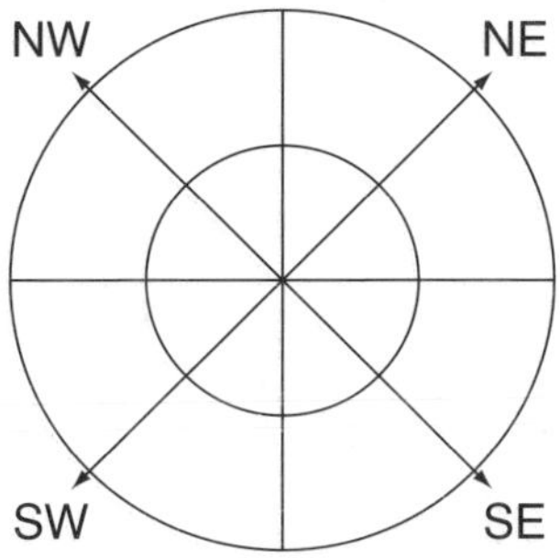

2. Which is the odd one out?

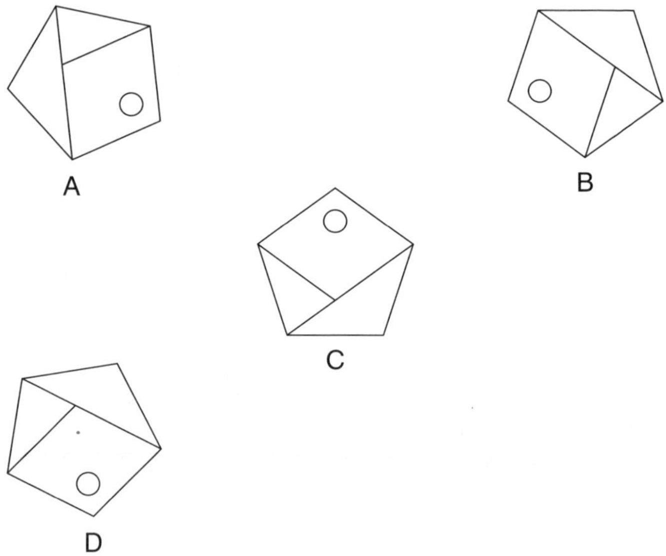

3. Solve the cryptic clue. The answer is an 11-letter word anagram within the clue:

inspect tiny article puzzlingly

4. What number should replace the question mark?

78214 : 292

38421 : 459

69517 : ?

5.

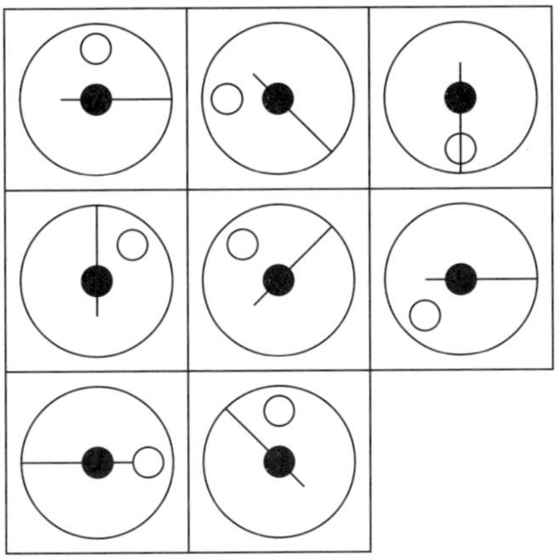

Which is the missing square?

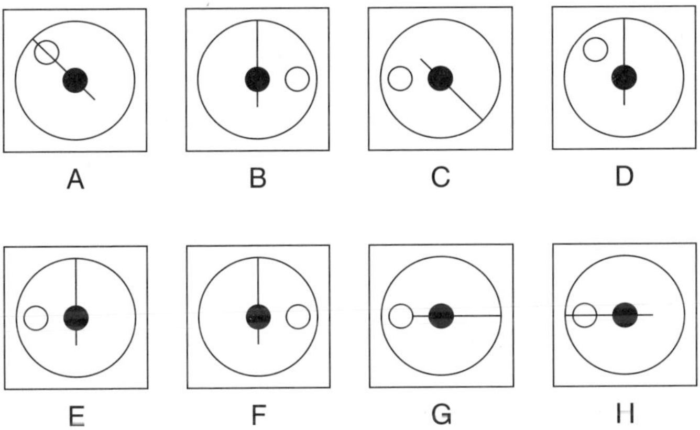

6. emancipate is to slavery as liberate is to: domination, burden, duty, responsibility, captivity

7. Insert two letters into each set of brackets so that they finish the word on the left and start the word on the right. The four pairs of letters inserted when read downwards in pairs will spell out an eight-letter word.

MA (**) AR

TE (**) ID

PI (**) RT

TI (**) AL

8. Midway through his round a golfer hits a magnificent 210-yard drive, which brings his average length per drive for the round up to now from 156 to 162 yards. How far would he have had to hit the drive to bring his average length of drive up from 156 to 165 yards?

9. 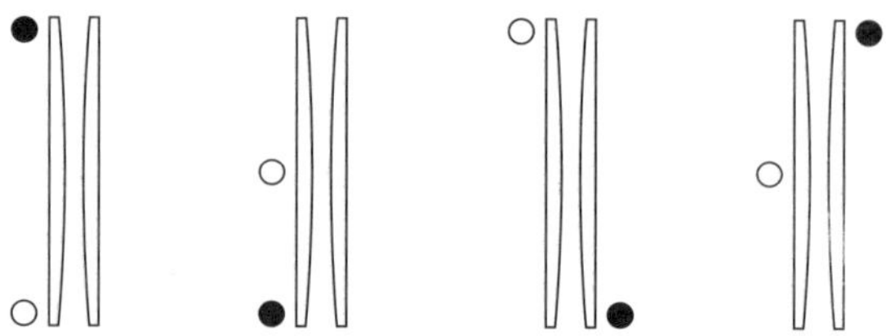

What comes next?

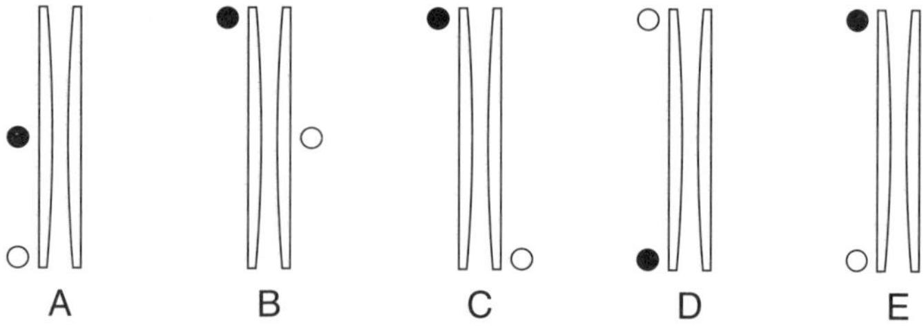

10. Which is the odd one out?

    segment, aggregate, ensemble, compliment, plenitude

11. Which two rhyming words mean smash garden tool?

12. Tom and Harry share a certain sum of money in the ratio 3 : 5. If Harry has £240, how much money is shared?

13. 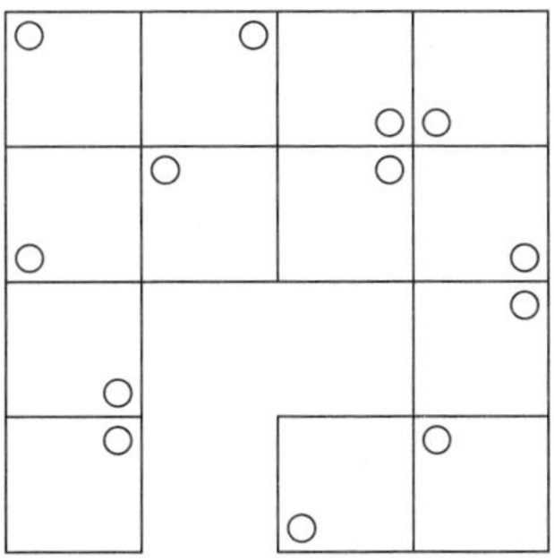

    Which is the missing segment?

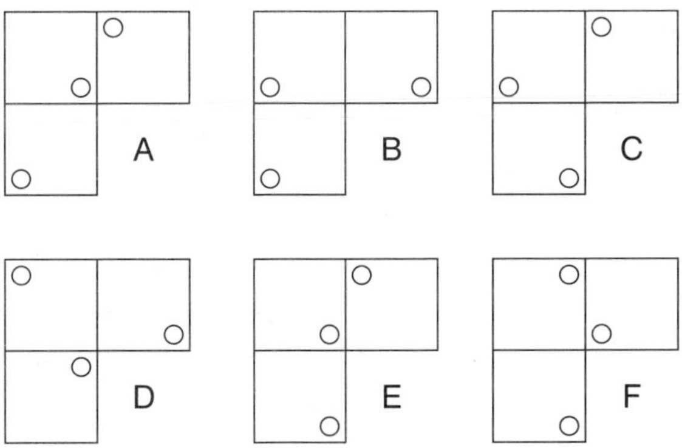

14. Which of the following is not an anagram of a job or profession?

    rein gene lee crock can chime mean lass no treaty

15. What number should replace the question mark?

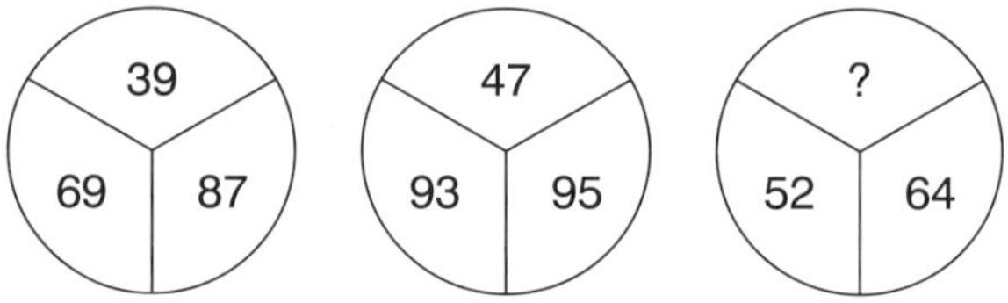

16. Which is the odd one out?

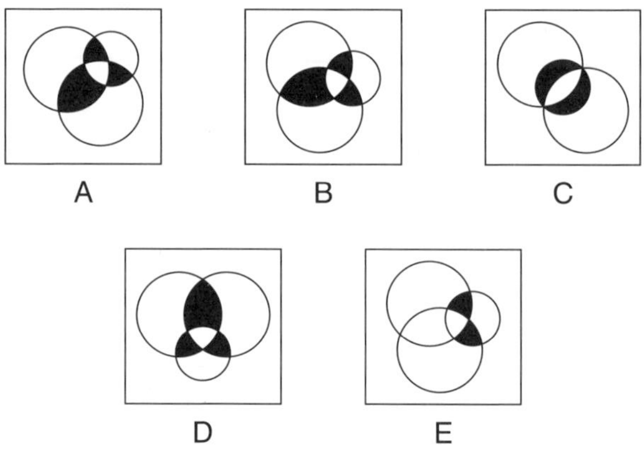

17. Seven synonyms of the keyword TREMENDOUS are listed. Take one letter in turn from each of the seven synonyms to spell out a further synonym of the keyword.

    great, terrific, monstrous, vast, enormous, gigantic, colossal

18. Which set of letters is the odd one out?

LMNQP EFGJI RSTWV IJKON OPQTS

19.

5	4	8	1	7
1	7	3	2	7
9	3	4	6	5
8	9	4	6	8
6	2	4	1	2

5	1	9	8	3
8	2	4	8	1
7	6	1	2	9
7	4	2	6	7
3	7	5	1	9

Find a string of four numbers in the first grid that also appears as a string of four numbers in the same order in the second grid. However, in each grid the string of four numbers may appear reading forwards, backwards, vertically, horizontally or diagonally.

20. 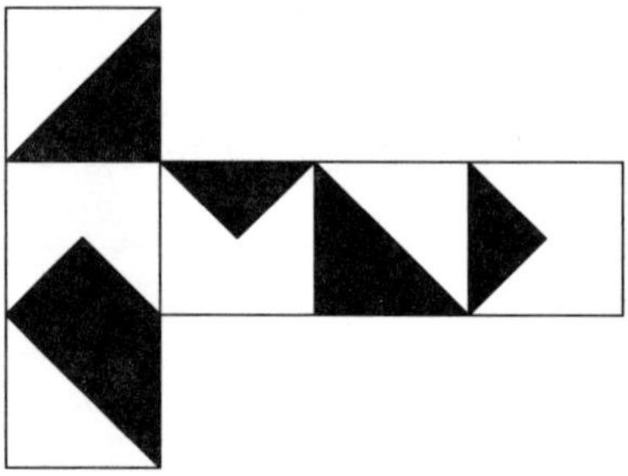

When the above is folded to form a cube, just one of the following can be produced. Which one?

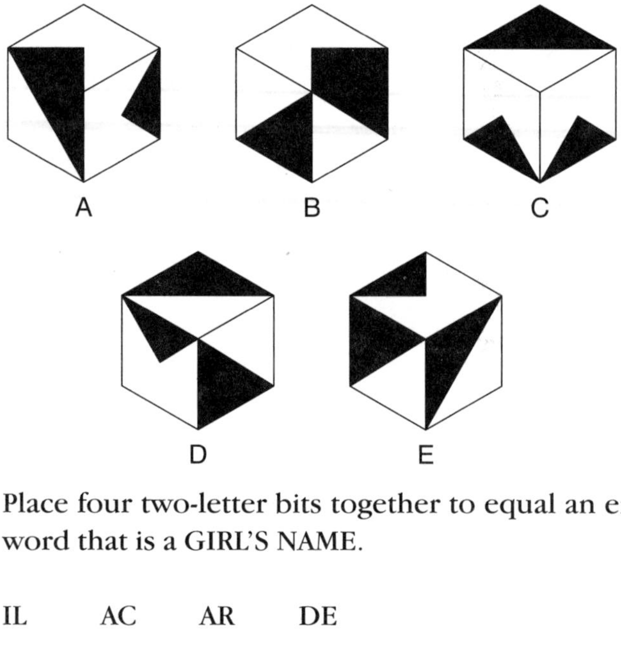

21. Place four two-letter bits together to equal an eight-letter word that is a GIRL'S NAME.

IL	AC	AR	DE
AB	FO	LA	EL

22. What is ASININE?

a. resembling an ass; b. having artistic leanings;

c. ear ache; d. dry;

e. drowsy.

23. What word can be prefixed to these words to make new words?

TAIL WHEEL KING PRICK NED

24. Which of these is not an anagram of a VEGETABLE?

RROTAC KINHGRE WORRMA TTAOPO KULIAS

25. Fill in the blanks to find two words that are SYNONYMS (clockwise or anticlockwise).

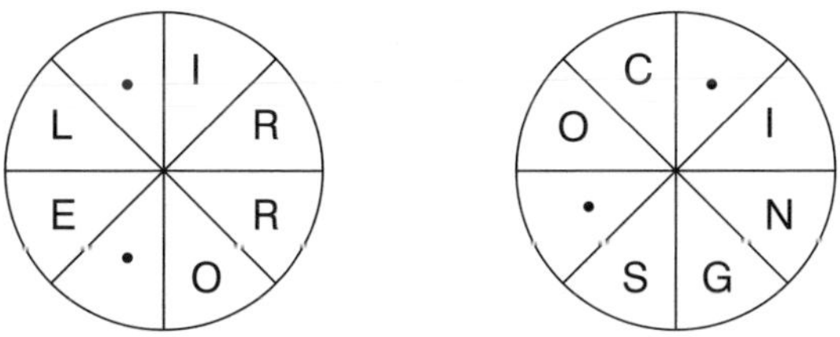

26. Find the value of the question mark.

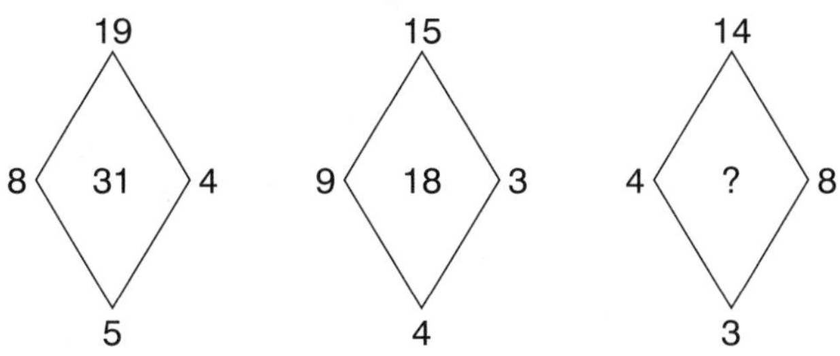

27. Fill in the two blanks and find a 12-letter word anagram that is a trade in rural areas.

O	U	T	R
L	•	H	U
R	E	•	I

28. What number should replace the question mark?

AVIATOR = 6

FIXTURE = 9

WIZARDS = 1

DIVERSE = ?

29. Insert a word that completes the first word and starts the second word.

QUICK (– – – –) BAG

30. Each of the nine squares in the grid marked 1A to 3C should incorporate all the lines and symbols that are shown in the squares of the same letter and number immediately above and to the left. For example, 2B should incorporate all the lines and symbols that are in 2 and B.

One of the squares is incorrect. Which one is it?

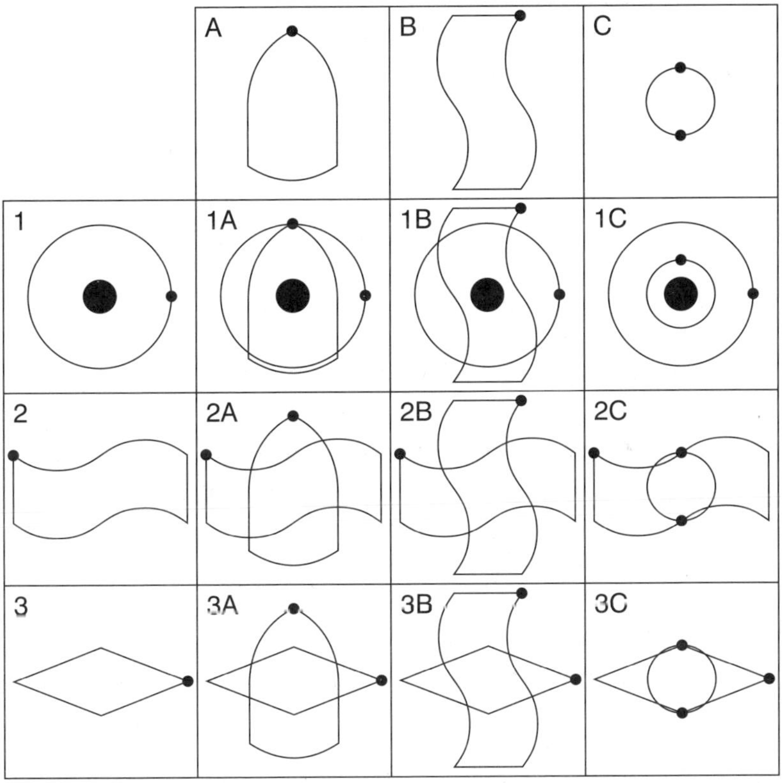

31. What number should replace the question mark?

71	63	4	2	19
32	8	16	25	34
9	12	43	61	7
4	35	26	18	?

32. Place two four-letter bits together to equal an eight-letter word that is a GAME.

FOOT OSTE LACR CLUB GHTS

HIGE GOLE DRAU JUMP BALE

33. What do these words have in common?

AVENUE RADIO GEMSTONE TAPPETS BANDED SIRIUS

34. Add three consecutive letters of the alphabet to the group of letters below, without splitting the consecutive letters, to form a word.

PALY

35. Place a word in the brackets that means the same as the two words outside the brackets.

LONG TAPERED STICK (– – –) PIG TAIL

36. What have these words got in common?

INFLICTED ESTEEM DENIAL CENTRED MADE

37. 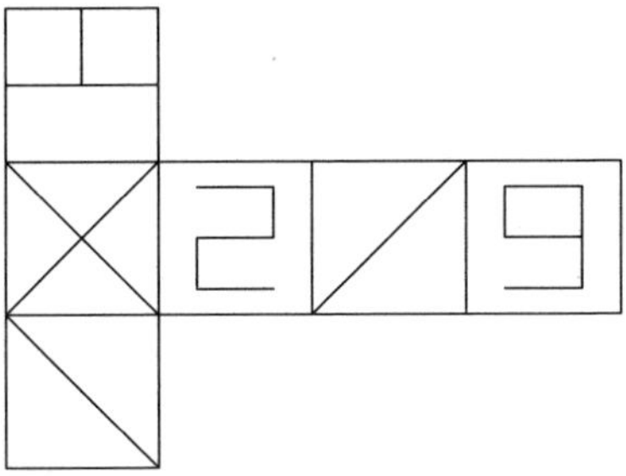

When the above is folded to form a cube, which is the only one of the following that *cannot* be produced?

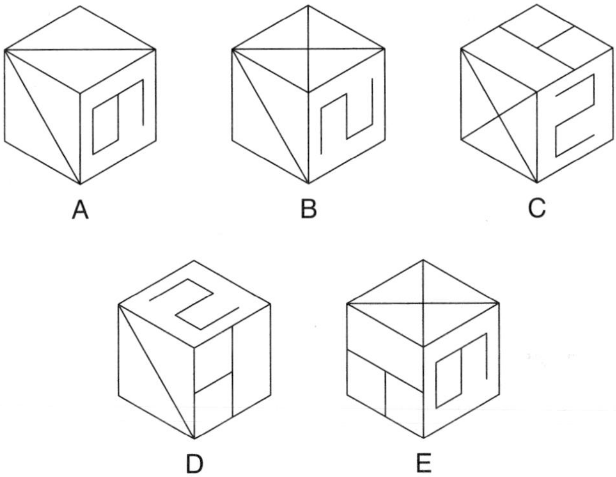

38. What country is missing from the brackets as in the example?

blade (Bangladesh) gnash

lover (– – – – – – – – – – –) salad

39. Which circle does not contain letters that will make a word?

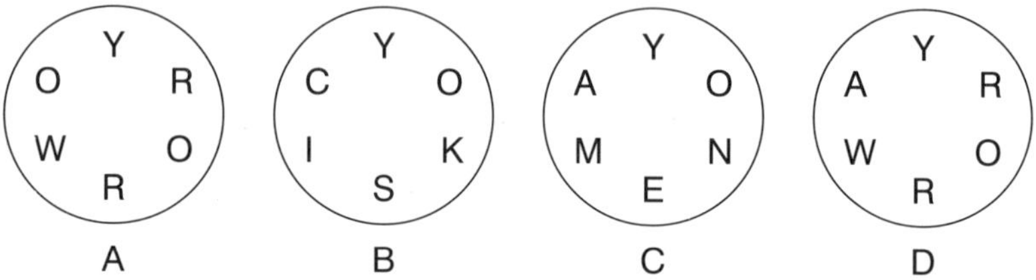

40. Letters are traced across the circle by chords. If the next letter is four letters or less away it will be found by tracing around the circumference.

Clue: DEFINITELY A WINTER'S BIRD (two words, four and five letters)

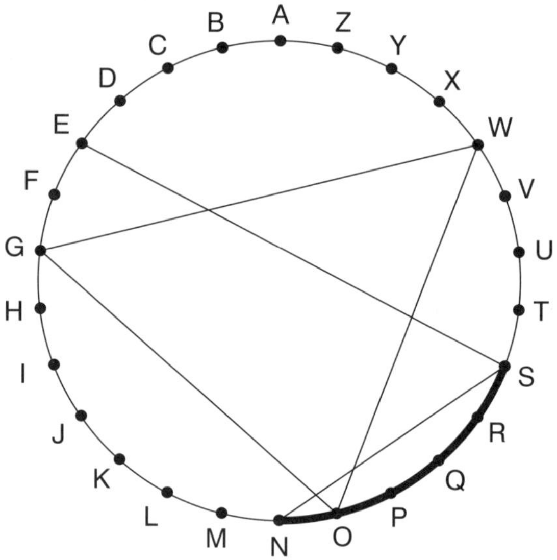

Test Five: Answers

1. BETRAYAL DEVOTION

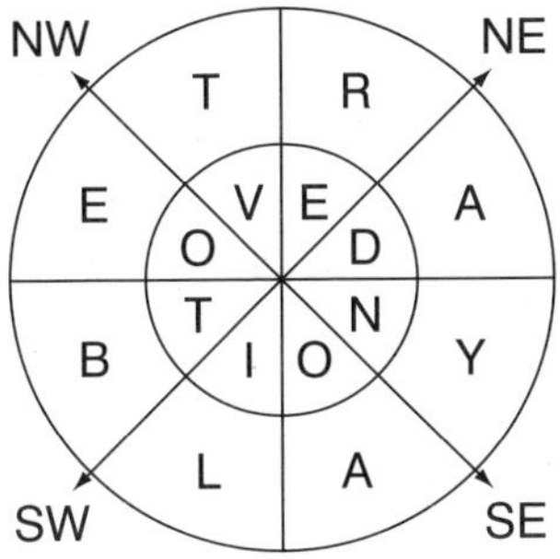

2. D: the rest are all the same figure rotated.

3. intricately (tiny article)

4. 586: 69 + 517 = 586

5. E: looking down, the line is moving 90 degrees anticlockwise and the white circle is moving 45 degrees clockwise. Looking across, the line is moving 45 degrees clockwise and the white circle is moving 90 degrees anticlockwise.

6. captivity

7. STAMPEDE: to give MAST/STAR TEAM/AMID PIPE/PERT and TIDE/DEAL.

8. 237 yards:

   eight holes average 156 = 1,248 yards

   nine holes average 162 = 1,458 yards (+ 210)

   nine holes average 165 = 1,485 yards (+ 237)

9. E: the black dot is moving round the two verticals clockwise top/bottom/bottom/top. The white dot is moving up and down the first vertical by half its length each time.

10. segment: it is a part, the rest are whole.

11. break rake

12. £384. Harry's share is £240 ie, each part is £48 (£240 ÷ 5). Therefore, the original amount was £48 × 8 (parts) (3 + 5) = £384

13. C: looking across, the dot is moving from corner to corner clockwise. Looking down, it is moving from corner to corner anticlockwise.

14. lee crock = cockerel. The jobs/professions are: engineer = rein gene, mechanic = can chime, salesman = mean lass and attorney = no treaty.

15. 29: 52 + 64 = 116. 116 ÷ 4 = 29. Similarly 93 + 95 = 188. 188 ÷ 4 = 47.

16. E: in all the others all areas common to two circles are shaded. In E, one such area is not.

17. titanic

18. IJKON: the rest are in the sequence three consecutive letters of the alphabet, then miss a letter, then reverse the next two.

19. 7462/2647

20. A.

21. ARABELLA

22. a. resembling an ass

23. PIN

24. SALUKI (dog). The others are CARROT; GHERKIN; MARROW; POTATO.

25. HORRIBLE SHOCKING

26. 34: 19 – 8 = 11 15 – 9 = 6 14 – 4 = 10

19 – 8 = 11	15 – 9 = 6	14 – 4 = 10
4 × 5 = 20	4 × 3 = 12	3 × 8 = 24
11 + 20 = 31	6 + 12 = 18	10 + 24 = 34

27. HORTICULTURE

28. 4: take the Roman numeral value of the second/third letters:

    A**VI**ATOR; F**IX**TURE; W**I**ZARDS; D**IV**ERSE

29. SAND

30. 1C

31. 23: the third line is the first line of figures reversed. The fourth line is the second line of figures reversed.

32. DRAUGHTS

33. They all carry girls' names backwards EVA, IDA, MEG, PAT, EDNA, IRIS

34. PANOPLY

35. CUE

36. They can all be prefixed with SELF-.

37. A

38. El Salvador (an anagram of lover, salad as Bangladesh is an anagram of blade, gnash)

39. A (B = YOICKS; C = YEOMAN; D = YARROW)

40. SNOW GOOSE

Test Six: Questions

1. Which is the odd one out?

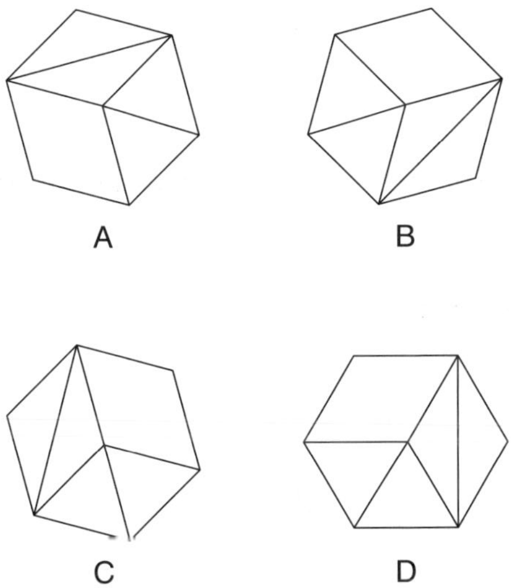

2. Which two words are closest in meaning?

   functional, vestigial, rudimentary, proficient, disappointing, savage

3. Find a word that when tacked onto the end of the first word produces another word or phrase and when placed in front of the second word produces another word or phrase.

   WELL   OUT

4. What number should replace the question mark?

3	8	6	36
7	4	2	14
6	8	4	48
9	6	2	?

5. Change one letter only in each word to produce a familiar phrase.

   so might say on

6. Which line of figures is the odd one out?

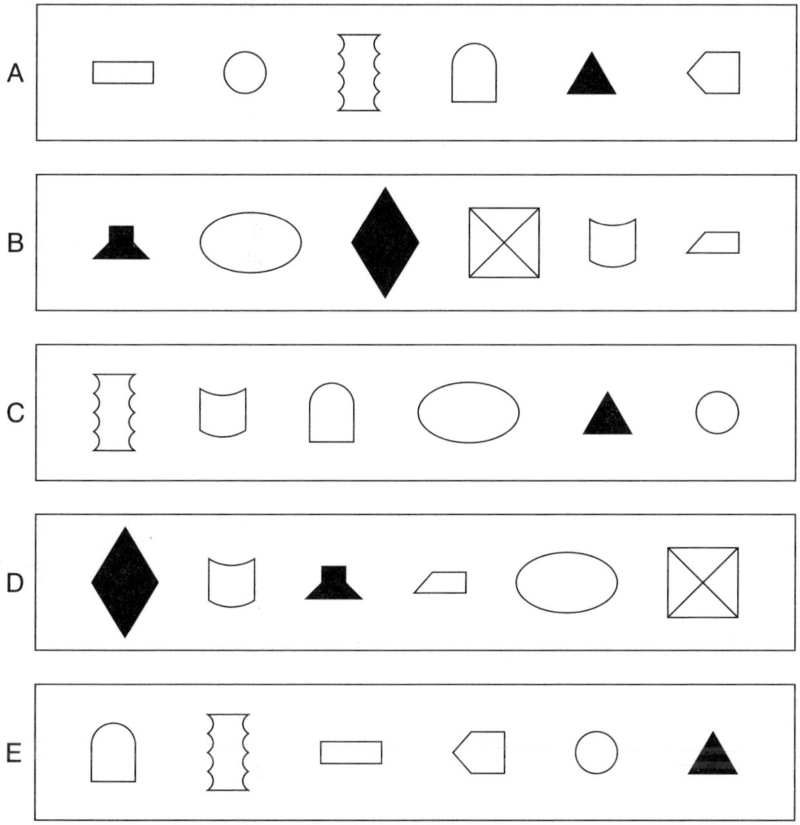

7. What number should replace the question mark?

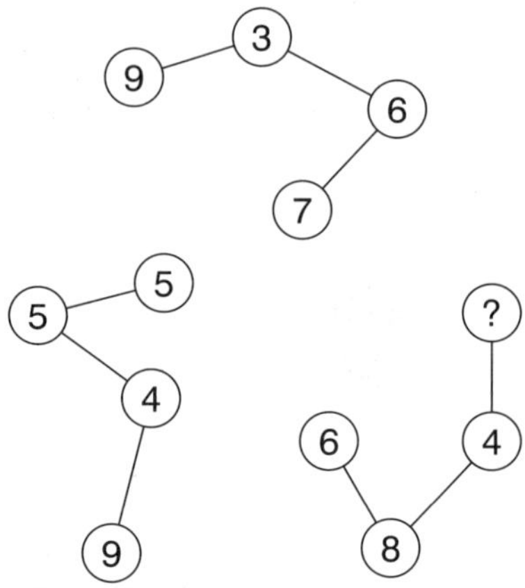

8.

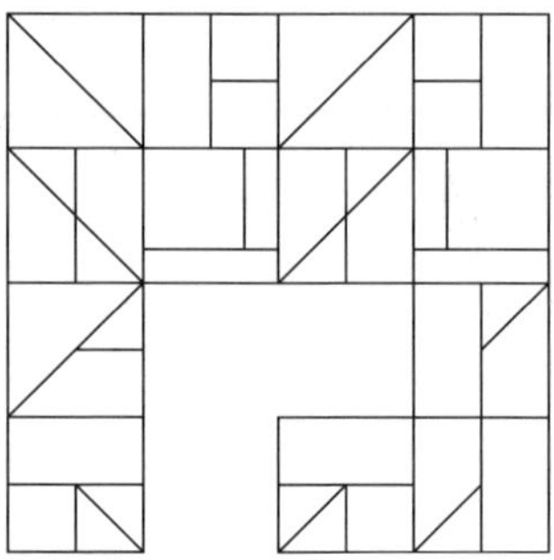

Which is the missing segment?

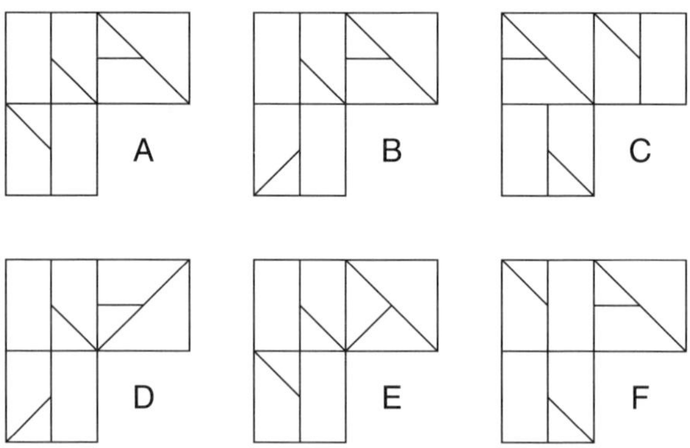

9. Which word in brackets is most opposite to the word in capitals?

   IMPECUNIOUS (accessible, tolerant, affluent, flawed, mortal)

10. Solve the anagram in brackets (12-letter word) to complete the quotation by Alfred North Whitehead.

    We think in (agile entries); we live in detail.

11.

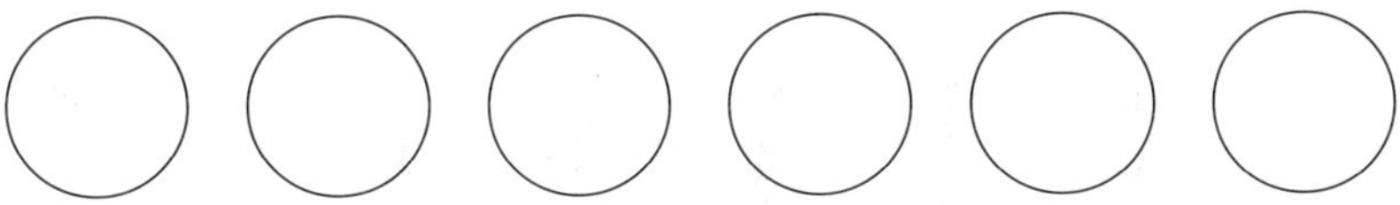

Insert the numbers 1–6 inclusive in the circles so that:

the sum of the numbers 4 and 5 and all the numbers in between = 19;

the sum of the numbers 6 and 3 and all the numbers in between = 10;

the sum of the numbers 2 and 1 and all the numbers in between = 11;

the sum of the numbers 4 and 3 and all the numbers in between = 14.

12.  is to 

as 

is to

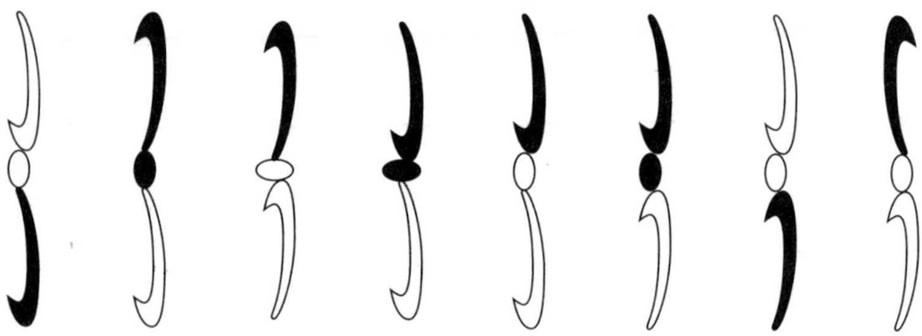

A B C D E F G H

13. Which is the odd one out?

devise, contemplate, contrive, design, concoct

14. Solve the anagrams to find one word that is opposite in meaning to the rest.

rude tie   no rating   dear Len   elite art

15. Which number is the odd one out?

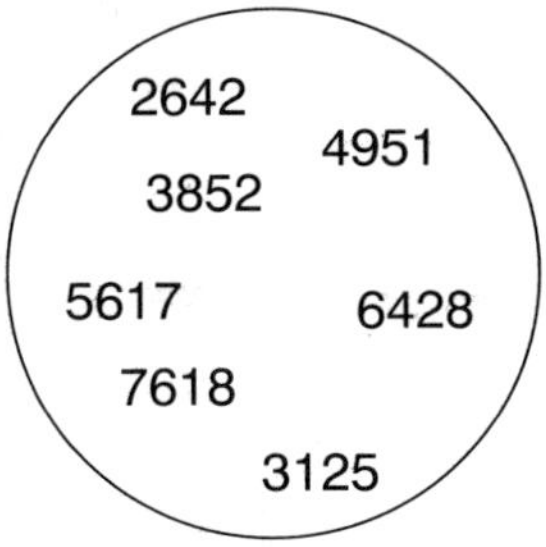

16.

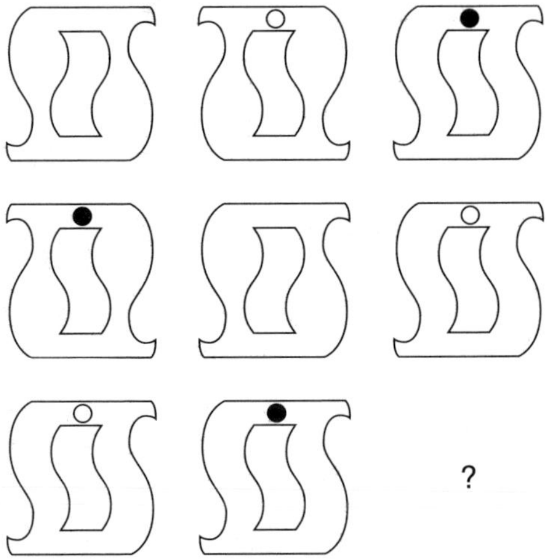

Which figure should replace the question mark?

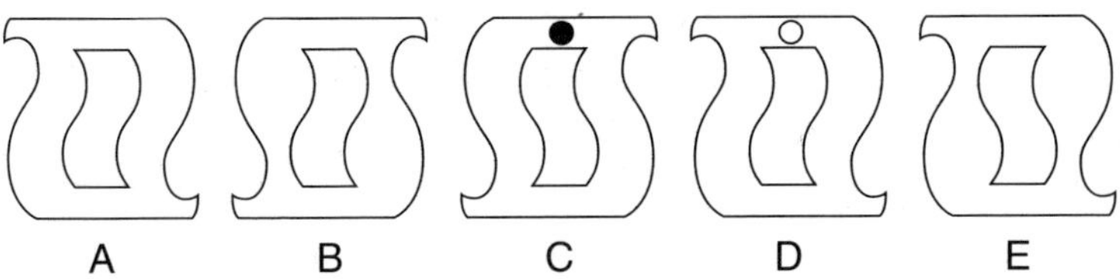

17. expert is to maven as novice is to: votary, sibling, tyro, boffin, scholar

18. What is the longest word that can be produced from the following 10 letters?

MUERVHANYL

19. What number should replace the question mark?

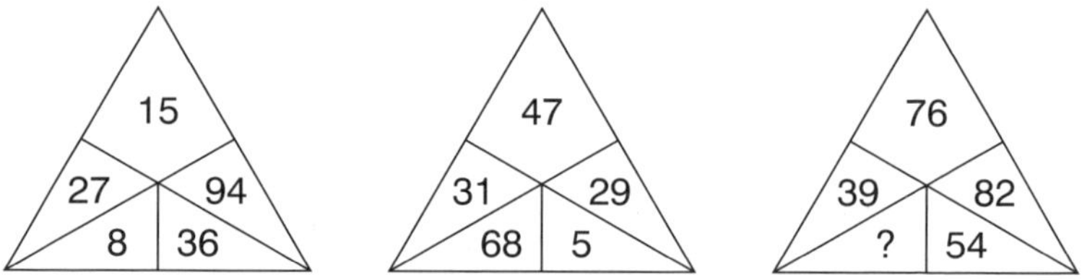

20.

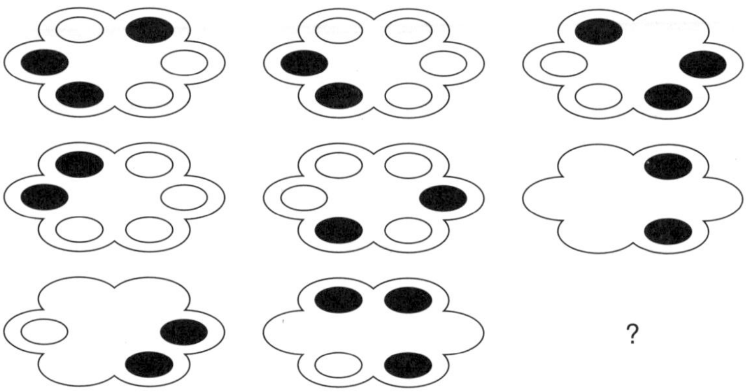

Which figure should replace the question mark?

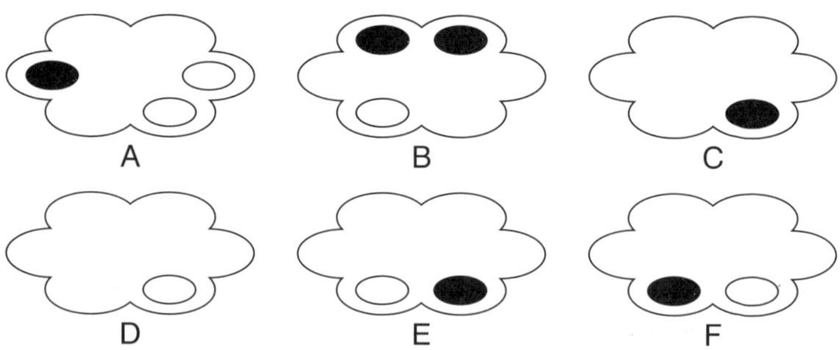

21. Crack the code to find a trite saying:

ZZGIH JLAMS ULKBV XSSAN PCDIM OBEES

UBJKV XOIAN PSVIQ STUVJ LSTCC

22. Find four sets of four numbers, each one totalling 200.

16	11	1	33
34	18	105	66
60	96	12	30
121	76	99	22

23. Place three two-letter bits together to equal a REPTILE.

IG AN CA NI UA YM

24. What number should replace the question mark?

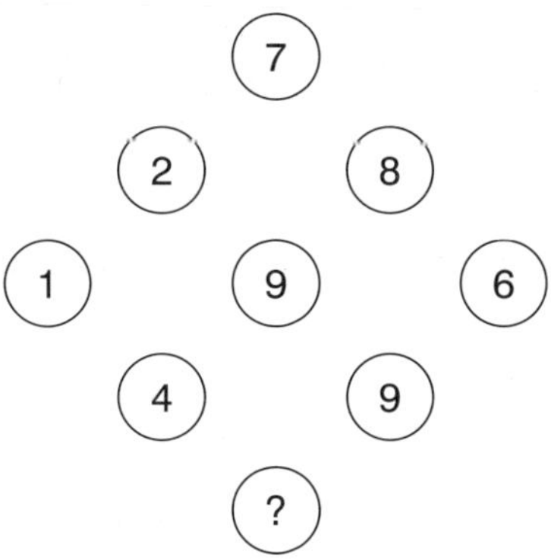

25. Arrange the letters to find two fish.

A E G G

I M N O

O U T T

26. What weight should be placed at ? to make the scale balance?

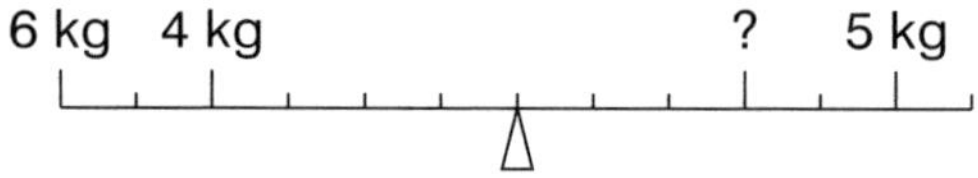

27. Place four two-letter bits together to equal an eight-letter BUILDING TERM.

ME NA AB RO

MA UT IC NT

28. Fill in the blanks and find two words that are ANTONYMS (clockwise or anticlockwise).

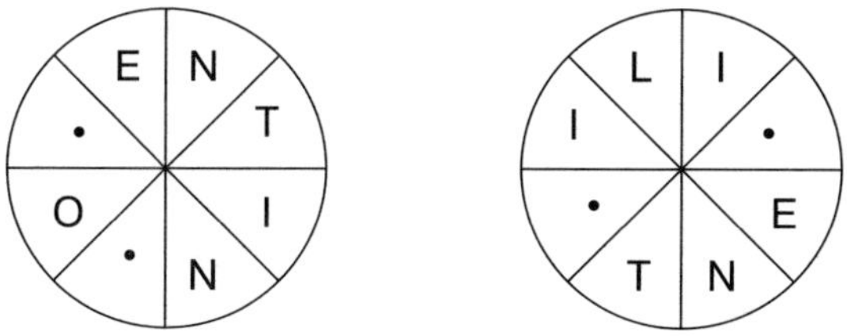

29. What is a CURRICLE?

a. a type of cabbage;

b. a light carriage;

c. a light framework;

d. a small boat.

30. Letters are traced across the circle by chords. If the next letter is four letters or less away it will be found by tracing around the circumference.

Clue: SOLO FLIGHT!

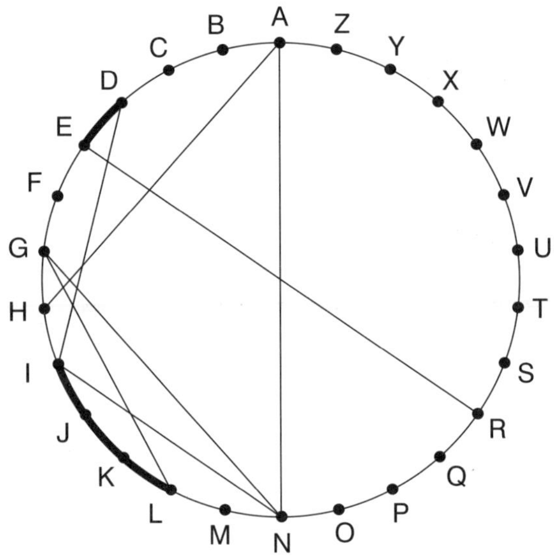

31.

12	9	14	10
15	34	5	11
7	4	3	23
26	13	16	18

In the arrangement of numbers above, what is the difference between the sum of the two highest odd numbers and the product of the two lowest even numbers?

32. What phrase is indicated below?

P

R

E T T

Y

33. Which is the odd one out?

a. PAVANE

b. COURANTE

c. JACINTH

d. GAVOTTE

e. RONDE

34. Find a one-word anagram for NEAT FILM.

35. Which word means the opposite of GUTTURAL?

a. vacillation; b. baleful;

c. germane; d. mellow.

36.

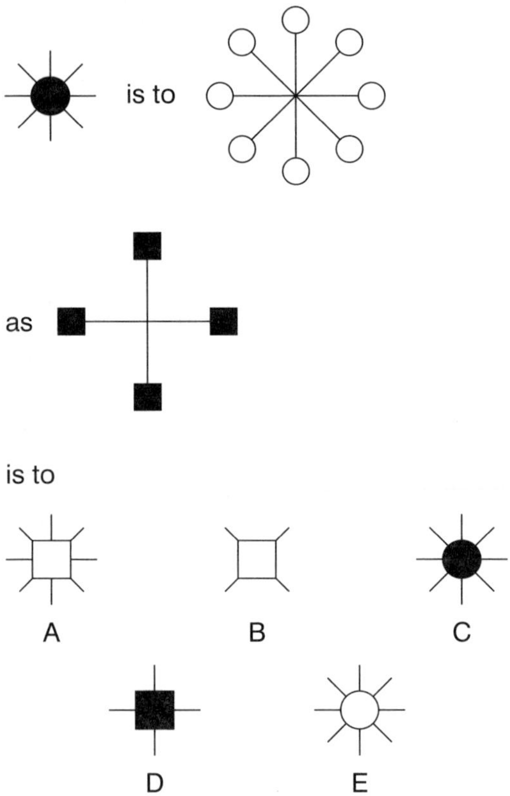

37. Change one letter in each word to get three words that are members of the same category. For example, foul, sax, tin = four, six, ten.

    weed, dab, near

38. What is RECTILINEAR?

    a. backwards;
    b. lying down;
    c. forming a semi-circle;
    d. forming a straight line;
    e. upright.

39. Which circle does not contain letters that will make up a word?

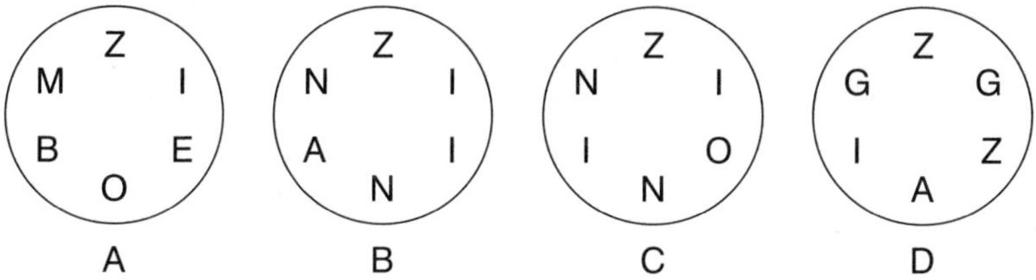

40. Letters are traced across the circle by chords. If the next letter is four letters or less away it will be found by tracing around the circumference.

Clue: IS THIS ANIMAL ONLY FOUND AT HIGH ALTITUDES? (12 letters)

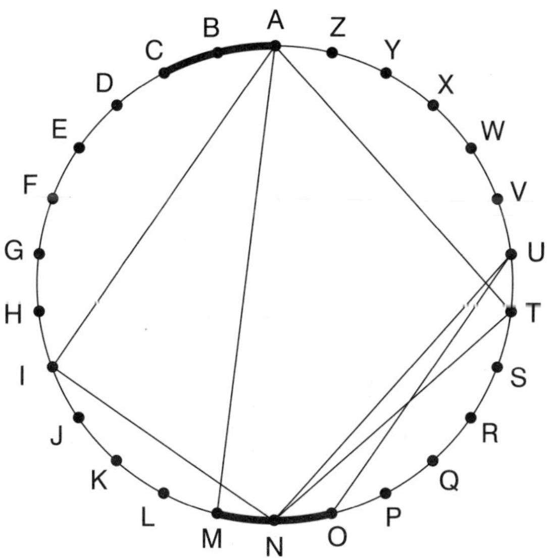

Test Six: Answers

1. C: the rest are the same figure rotated.

2. vestigial, rudimentary

3. READ

4. 27: halve the second and third numbers then multiply the first three numbers in each line to produce the fourth number, so $9 \times 3\ (6 \div 2) \times 1\ (2 \div 2) = 27$.

5. to fight shy of

6. C: A contains the same figures as E and B contains the same figures as D.

7. 8: multiply the two outside numbers to obtain the number formed by the middle two digits reversed.

8. F: so that the first column is a mirror image of the third column and the second column is a mirror image of the fourth column.

9. affluent

10. generalities

11. 4 6 1 3 5 2 or 2 5 3 1 6 4

12. H: the left-hand figure rotates 90 degrees clockwise and goes to the bottom. The right-hand figure rotates 90 degrees anticlockwise and goes to the top. The centre ellipse changes from black to white.

13. contemplate

14. ignorant = no rating. The synonyms are erudite = rude tie, learned = dear Len and literate = elite art.

15. 5617: in all the others, the third digit is the difference between the first and second digits and the first digit is the difference between the third and fourth digits.

16. A: each line and column contains the main figure once reversed, a white dot, a black dot and the internal figure once reversed.

17. tyro

18. HUMANELY

19. 1: each triangle contains the digits 1–9 once each only.

20. D: in each line and column ellipses are only carried forward to the third cloud when the same colour ellipse appears in the same position in the first two clouds; however, they then change from black to white and vice versa.

21. IT WON'T WORK (each letter is found in the space between the letters shown).

22. (66, 96, 22, 16) (99, 11, 60, 30) (1, 18, 76, 105) (33, 34, 12, 121)

23. CAYMAN

24. 4: from the top, $7 \times 28 = 196$ and from the bottom, $4 \times 49 = 196$

25. GOURAMI GOURNET

26. 9 kg. LH: $6\text{ kg} \times 6 = 36\text{ kg}$ RH: $5\text{ kg} \times 5 = 25\text{ kg}$

$4\text{ kg} \times 4 = 16\text{ kg}$ $9\text{ kg} \times 3 = 27\text{ kg}$

$36 + 16 = 52\text{ kg}$ $25 + 27 = 52\text{ kg}$

27. ABUTMENT

28. INDOLENT DILIGENT

29. b. a light carriage

30. HANG GLIDER

31. 2: $4 \times 10 = 40$ and $23 + 15 = 38$

32. SITTING PRETTY

33. c. JACINTH (a reddish-orange gem). The others are dances.

34. FILAMENT

35. d. mellow

36. B: reversing the first analogy, the four black squares become one white square in the centre with four arms attached to it.

37. week, day, year

38. d. forming a straight line

39. C: (A = ZOMBIE; B = ZINNIA; D = ZIGZAG)

40. CATAMOUNTAIN

Test Seven: Questions

1.

Which is the missing section?

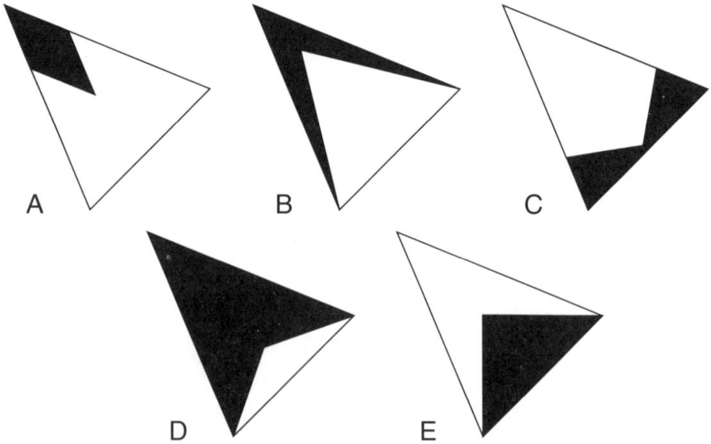

2. Add one letter, not necessarily the same letter, to the beginning, middle or end of each of these words to form two other words that are similar in meaning.

   tip   aunt

3. What letter comes next?

   A   D   H   K   O   ?

4. What numbers should replace the question marks?

   5   3   8   1   2   5

   7   2   2   4   9   3

   2   5   6   5   ?   ?

5. 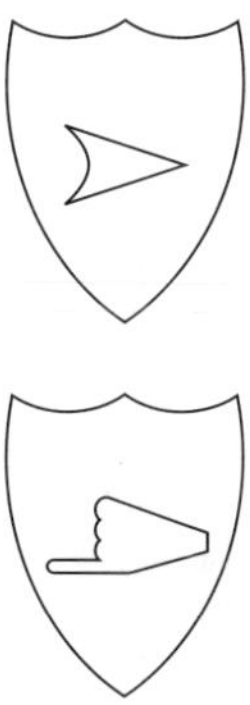

   Which is the missing shield?

   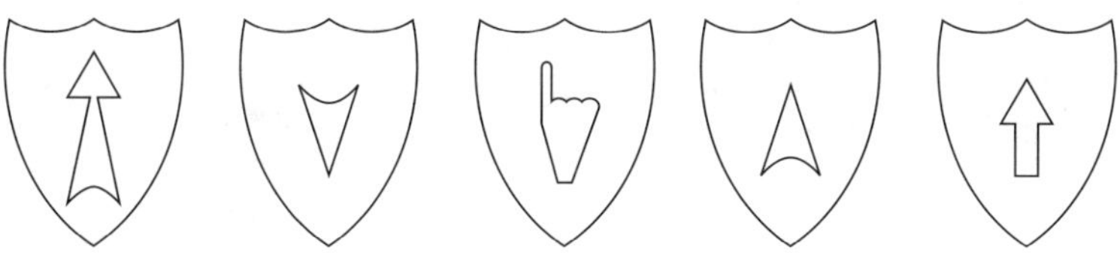

   A   B   C   D   E

6. CUBED RESULT is an anagram of which two words that are opposite in meaning?

7. surmise is to conjecture as axiom is to: custom, idea, concept, caprice, premise

8. What number should replace the question mark?

18	6	15	9
13	11	7	17
5	19	?	3
16	8	14	10

9. 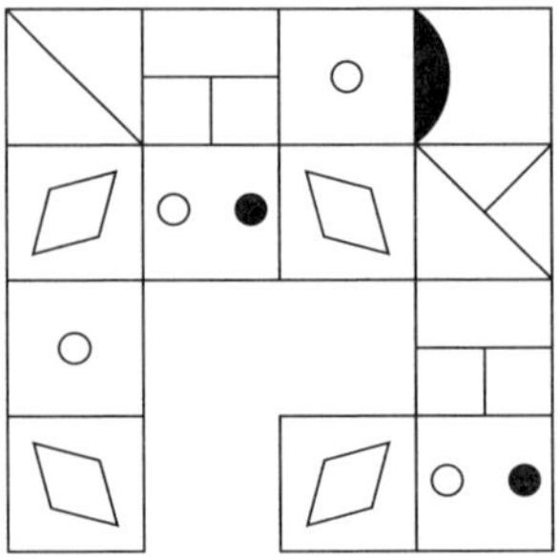

Which is the missing segment?

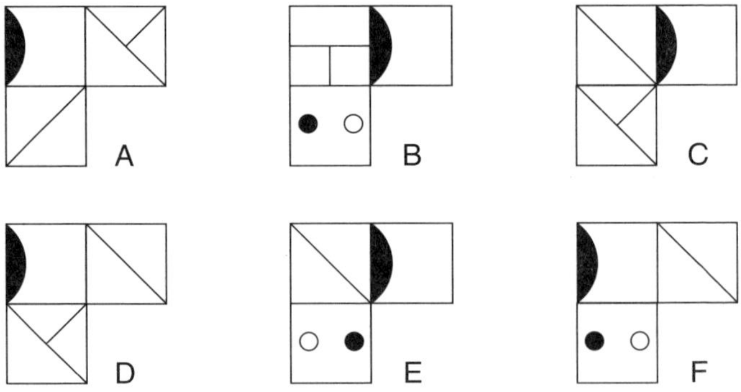

10. Which is the odd one out?

    lampoon, pillory, spoof, burlesque, skit

11. Which two rhyming words mean the same as DELIGHTFUL OFFERING?

12. What number should replace the question mark?

    3925 : 277

    4697 : 2416

    6257 : ?

13.

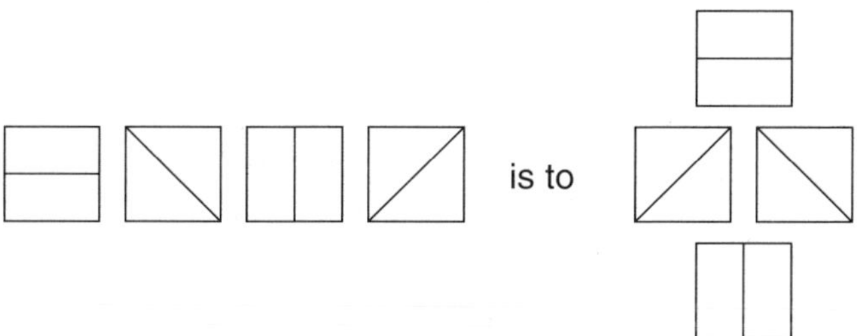

as

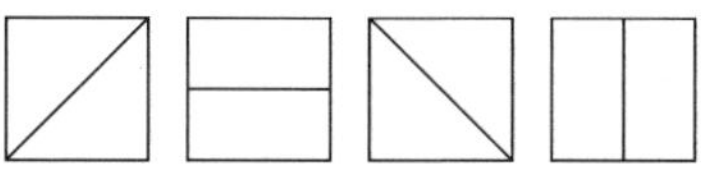

is to

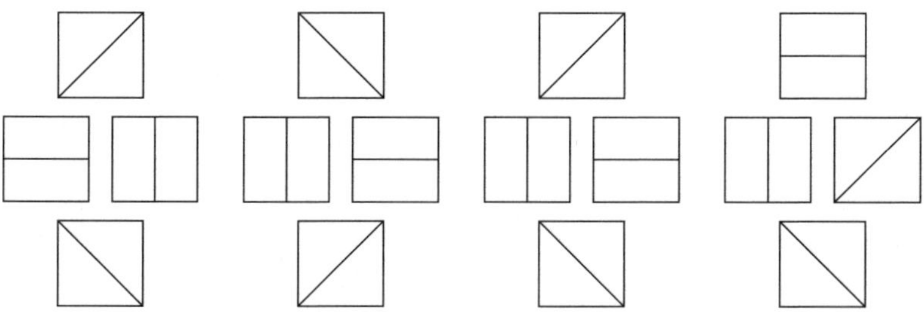

A B C D

14. Which of the following is not an anagram of a musical term?

    no baiter   rent coco   revue rot   rod arch   shop yard

15. Insert the missing number in each grid.

3	9	6	7
4	9		6
3	4	8	8
2	7	4	9

7	9	3	4
9	8	5	2
6	9	7	6
5	4	9	

16.

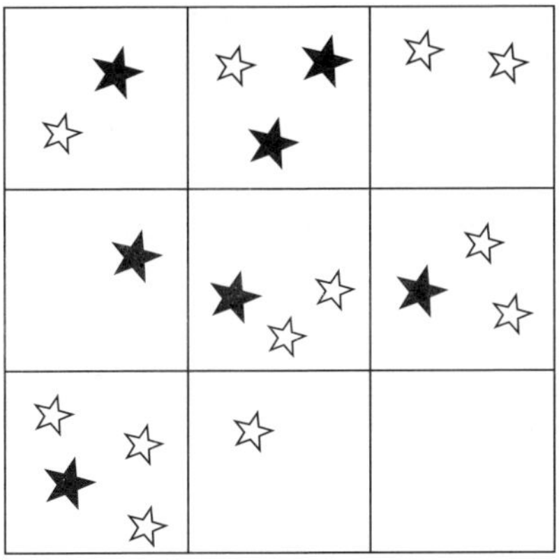

Which is the missing square?

A

B

C

D

E

F

G

H

17. NICE OLD NOUN is an anagram of which familiar phrase (two, five, four letters).

Clue: the height of bliss?

18. Kate has a quarter as many again as Peter and Peter has a third as many again as Jill. Altogether they have 120. How many has each?

19. Change one letter only in each word to produce a familiar phrase.

so dive I dot O bid came

20. 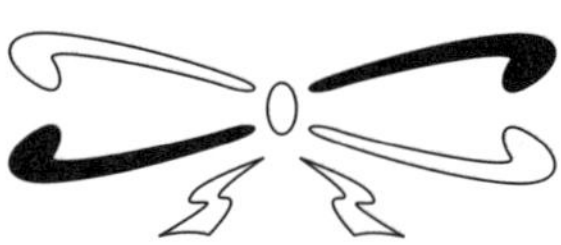 is to 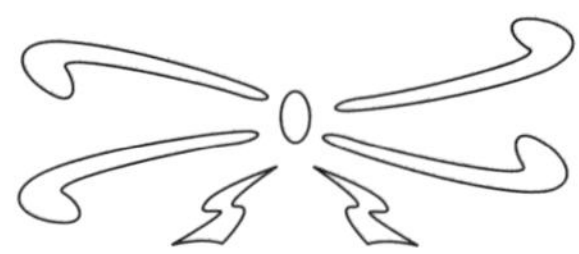

as

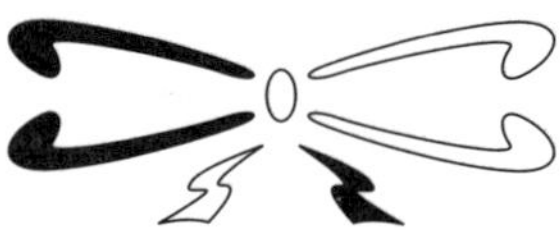

is to

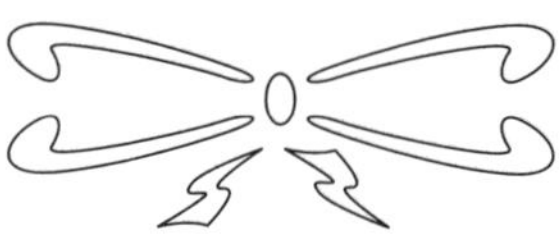

A

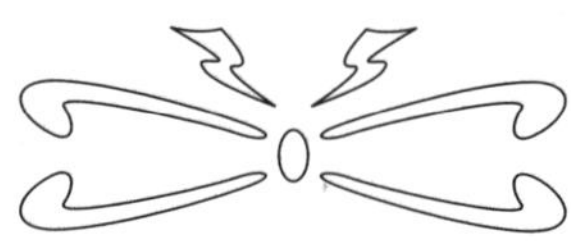

B

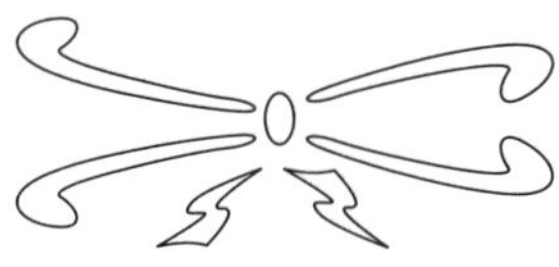

C

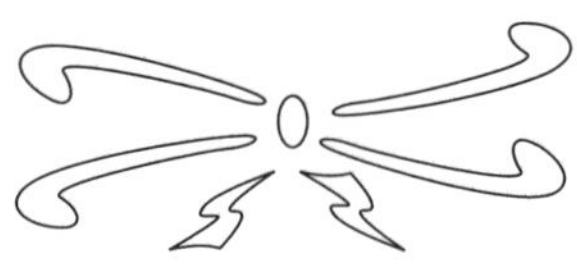

D

21. Which number is the odd one out?

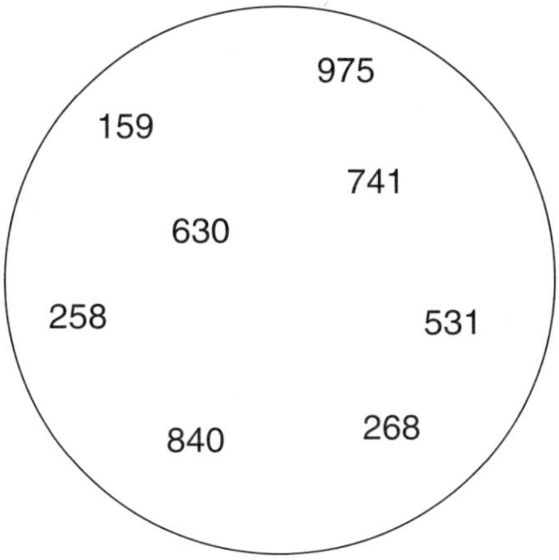

22. Which two words are most similar in meaning?

instability, inimitable, refusing, matchless, hostile, iniquity

23. Place two four-letter bits together to equal one eight-letter word that is an OCCUPATION.

SSOR BOWM ATTO BAND RNEI

SNAM SMAL ASSE BOAT ALER

24. Which of the following is not a COIN?

a. BETONY;

b. BOLIVAR;

c. CRUSADO;

d. MOIDORE.

25. Change one letter in each word to make DOGS.

    LURCHED TUMBLED FATTER DOODLE

26. Fill in the blanks to find two words that are ANTONYMS (clockwise or anticlockwise).

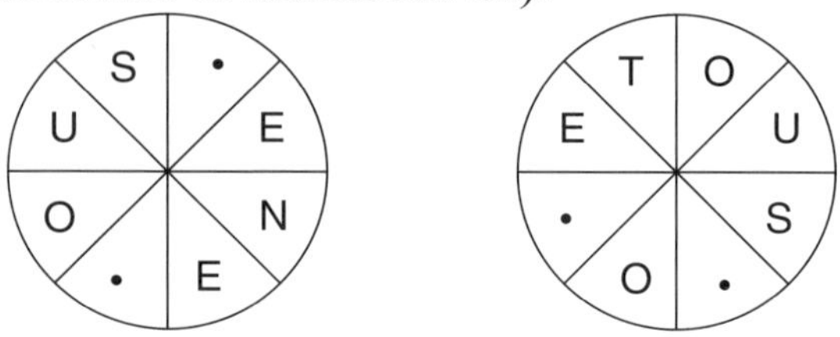

27. femur is to thigh as scapula is to: shoulder, skull, jaw, collar, skin

28. Visit each circle only once to spell out a 10-letter word.

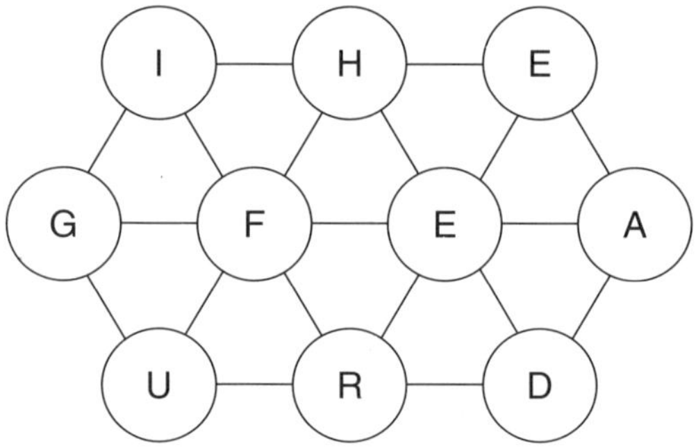

29. Fill in the blanks to find a word that is a colour (clockwise or anticlockwise).

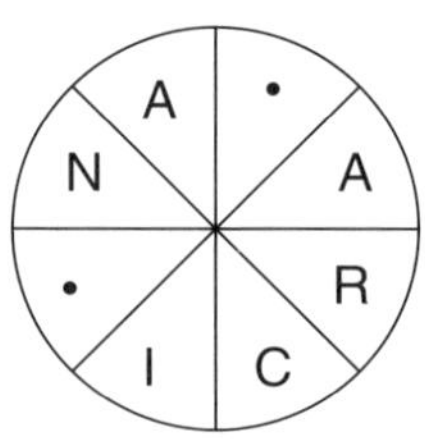

30. 4927 is to 575

and 3968 is to 632

therefore 2916 is to ?

31. Which two words have opposite meanings?

refractory, arbiter, rectitude, recumbent, propitiate, fatigue, sanctuary, obedient

32. Which is the odd one out?

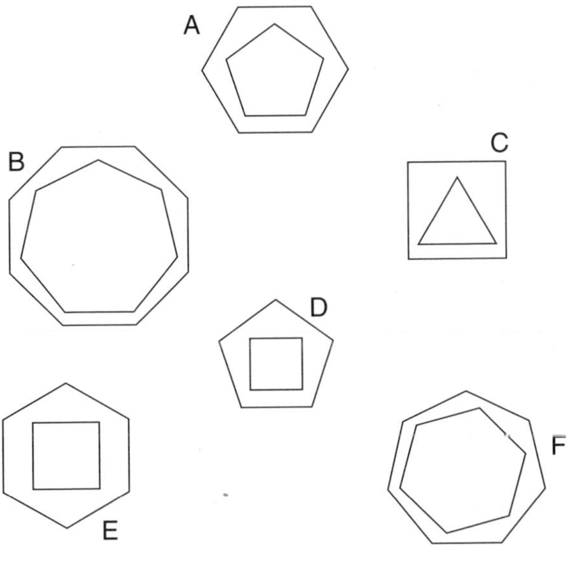

33. Which two words are the opposite in meaning:

overbearing, perverse, enervating, boundless, confronting, obsequious

34. What weight must be placed at ? to balance the scale?

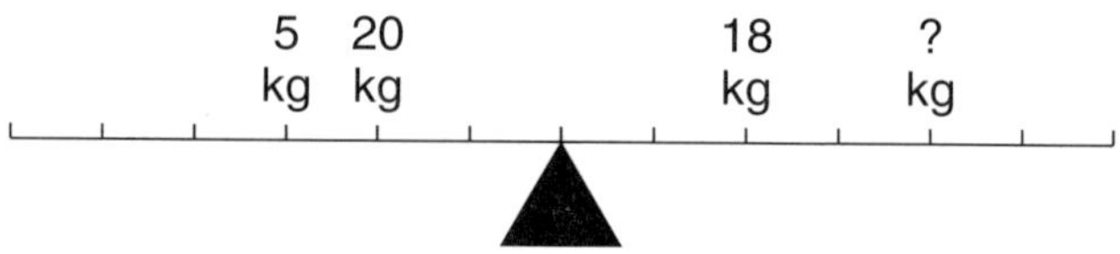

35. Which phrase means the same as soporific?

a. shyly indifferent;

b. sleep inducing;

c. very sorrowful;

d. deeply solemn.

36. What does the word PINCHBECK mean?

a. snuff;

b. a mixture of copper and zinc;

c. a granite wall;

d. a small town.

37. Fill in the blanks to find two words that are SYNONYMS (clockwise or anticlockwise).

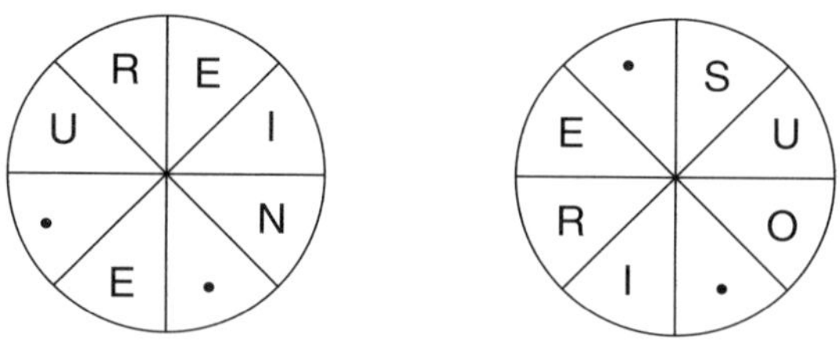

38. What does the word MÉTIER mean?

a. having mettle;

b. threatening;

c. mindful;

d. being minimus;

e. trade or profession.

39.

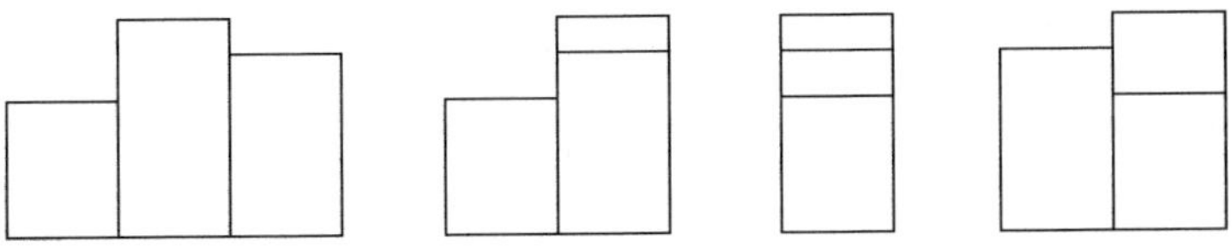

What comes next?

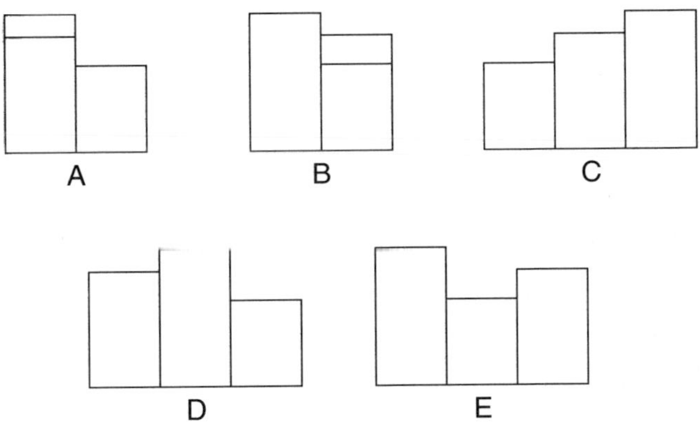

40. Letters are traced across the circle by chords. If the next letter is four letters or less away it will be found by tracing around the circumference.

Clue: SINGERS BUT ONLY IN THE EVENING? (12 letters)

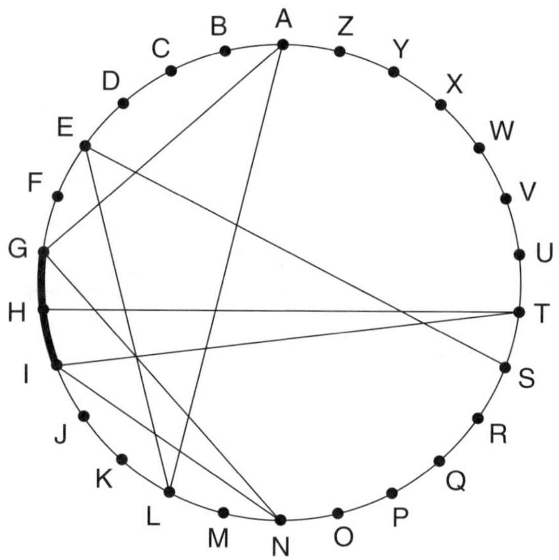

Test Seven: Answers

1. D: each segment is a mirror image of the segment opposite.

2. trip jaunt

3. R: skip two letters then three ie, AbcDefgHijKlmnOpqR

4. 7 8: looking down each column alternately, take the difference, then add, so, the difference between 2 and 9 = 7 and 5 + 3 = 8.

5. D: so that the four arrows are pointing North, South, East, West and opposite pointers are the same type ie, finger or arrow.

6. CRUDE, SUBTLE

7. premise

8. 21: pairs of numbers in lines reading across = 24

9. D: opposite corner blocks of four squares are identical.

10. pillory

11. pleasant present

12. 1212: $6 \times 2 = 12$, $5 + 7 = 12$. Similarly $4 \times 6 = 24$ and $9 + 7 = 16$ (2416).

13. C: the square on the left goes to the top, the square second left goes to middle right, the square second right goes to the bottom and the square on the right goes middle left.

14. rod arch = orchard. The musical terms are baritone = no baiter, concerto = rent coco, overture = revue rot and rhapsody = shop yard.

15. 2 in the left-hand square and 8 in the right-hand square. Each row of numbers in the left-hand square is multiplied by 2 to arrive at the row opposite in the right-hand square, i.e. $3967 \times 2 = 7934$

16. H: each row and column contains three black stars and four white stars.

17. ON CLOUD NINE

18. Jill 30, Peter 40, Kate 50

19. to give a dog a bad name

20. C: all white segments remain the same but black segments turn white and flip over.

21. 268: in all the others, the difference between the digits is the same, for example, with 159, 1 + 4 = 5 and 5 + 4 = 9.

22. inimitable, matchless

23. ASSESSOR

24. a. BETONY (a plant)

25. LURCHER, TUMBLER, RATTER, POODLE

26. GENEROUS COVETOUS

27. shoulder

28. FIGUREHEAD

29. CINNABAR

30. 785: take the difference between digits in the first number to obtain the second number. Thus 2916 produces 7 (the difference between 2 and 9) 8 (the difference between 9 and 1) 5 (the difference between 1 and 6).

31. refractory, obedient

32. E: in all the others, the number of sides on the figure in the middle is one less than the number of sides on the figure on the outside.

33. overbearing, obsequious

34. 4.75 kg: 5 kg × 3 = 15 kg 18 kg × 2 = 36 kg

20 kg × 2 = 40 kg 4.75 kg × 4 = 19 kg

15 kg + 40 kg = 55 kg 36 kg + 19 kg = 55 kg

35. sleep inducing

36. b. a mixture of copper and zinc

37. INSECURE PERILOUS

38. e. trade or profession

39. D: the figures originally on the left and right are moving one place to the right and left alternately at each stage.

40. NIGHTINGALES

Test Eight: Questions

1. What number should replace the question mark?

1		1			2	3	2
	4			2			3
2		2			2		2
	4			2			3
	3	5	3			4	3
	3		3		3	?	
1			2		3		2
		1				2	

2.

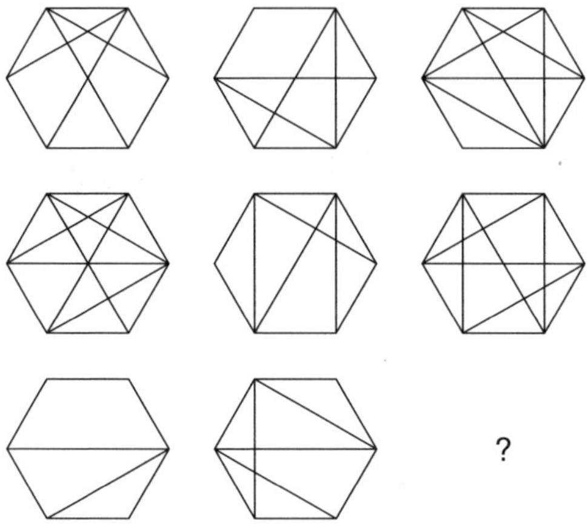

Which hexagon should replace the question mark?

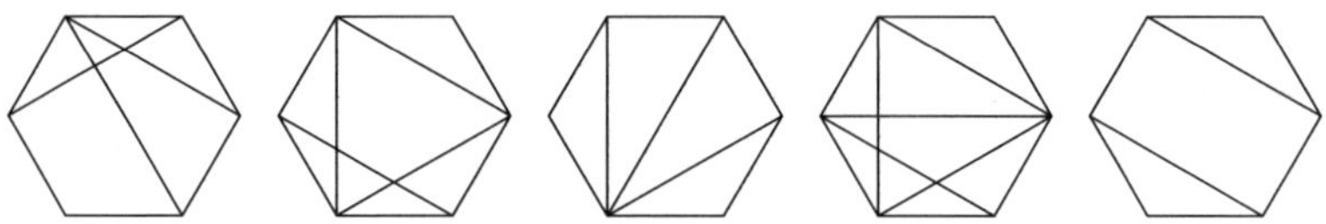

A B C D E

3. Restore the vowels to the row of letters below to spell out four words that are similar in meaning. All consonants are in the correct order.

D R C H R S H V N R T R V R

4. Insert the missing letters to spell out a familiar phrase reading clockwise. Only alternate letters are shown and you must find the starting point.

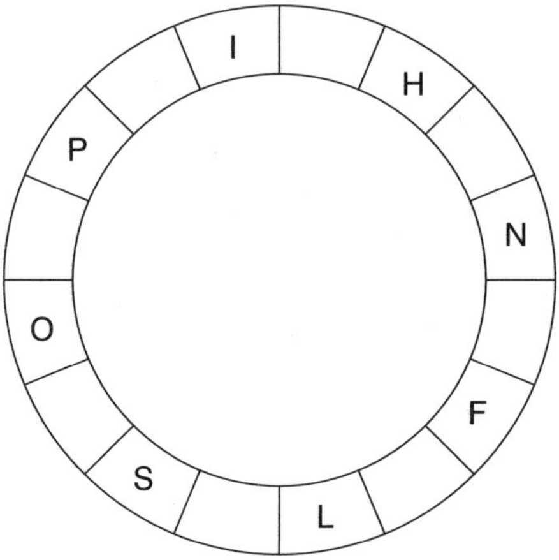

5.

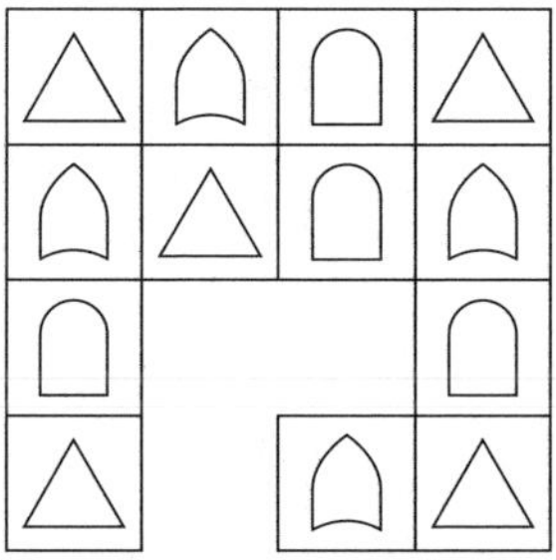

Which is the missing segment?

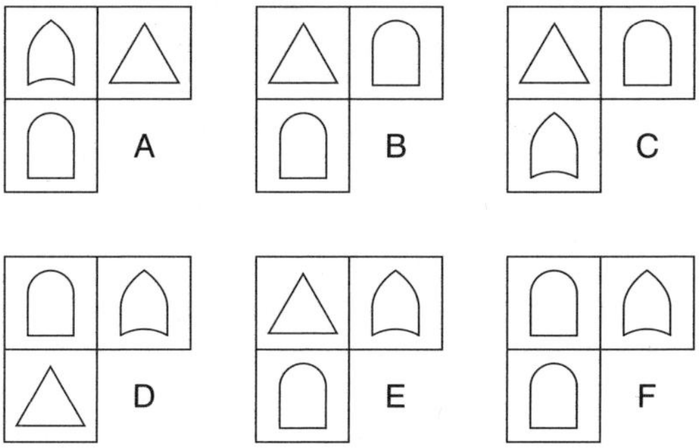

6. Find two words, one reading clockwise round one circle and the other anticlockwise round the other circle, which are antonyms. You must find the starting points and provide the missing letters.

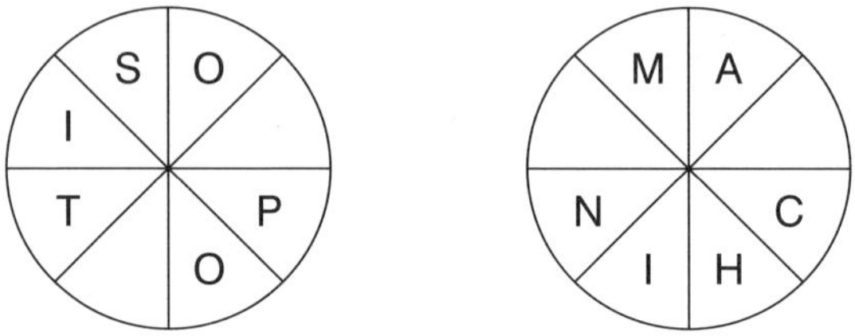

7. Only one set of five letters below can be rearranged to spell out a five-letter English word. Find the word.

GOZAM TROMC PLACT OECLR MUYJP
TANRO EFOLC

8. How many minutes is it before 12 noon if 90 minutes ago it was twice as many minutes past 8 am?

9. 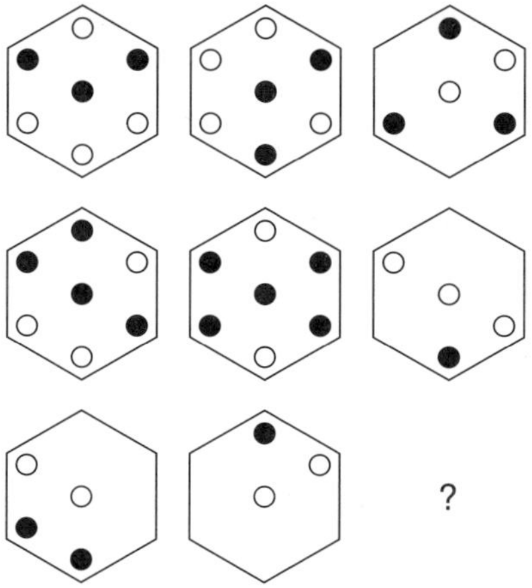

Which hexagon should replace the question mark?

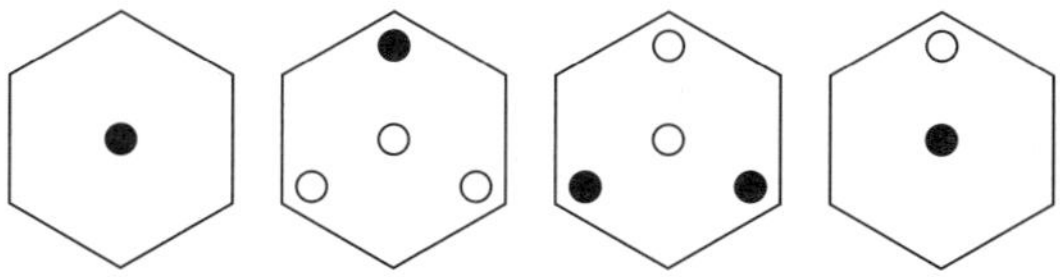

A B C D

10. Which is the odd one out?

drapes, realtor, fanlight, diaper, tuxedo

11. A B C D E F G H

Which letter is two to the right of the letter immediately to the left of the letter three to the right of the letter immediately to the right of the letter A?

12. What numbers should replace the question marks?

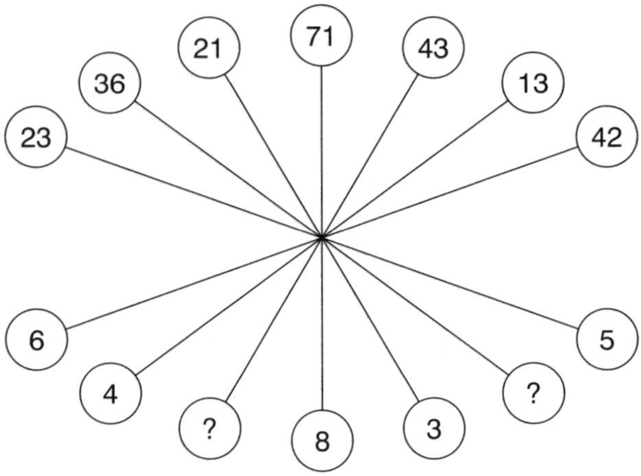

13.

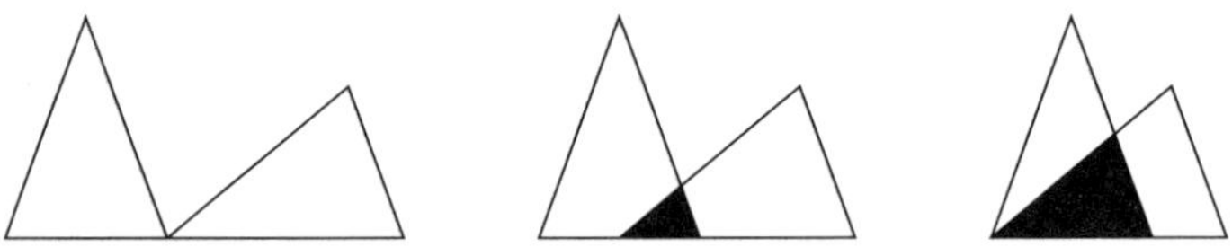

Which of the options below continues the above sequence?

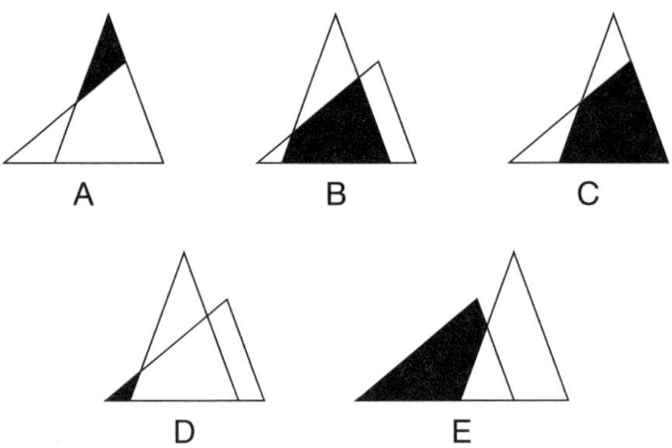

14. patella is to kneecap as sternum is to: collarbone, jawbone, thighbone, breastbone, shoulder-blade.

15. Start at one of the corner squares and spiral clockwise round the perimeter to spell out a nine-letter word, finishing at the centre. You must provide the missing letters.

N	I	N
E	*	S
*	L	U

16. If Tony's age + Cherie's age = 80 and Tony's age + Gordon's age = 98 and Cherie's age + Gordon's age = 94, how old are Tony, Cherie and Gordon?

17. Which is the odd one out?

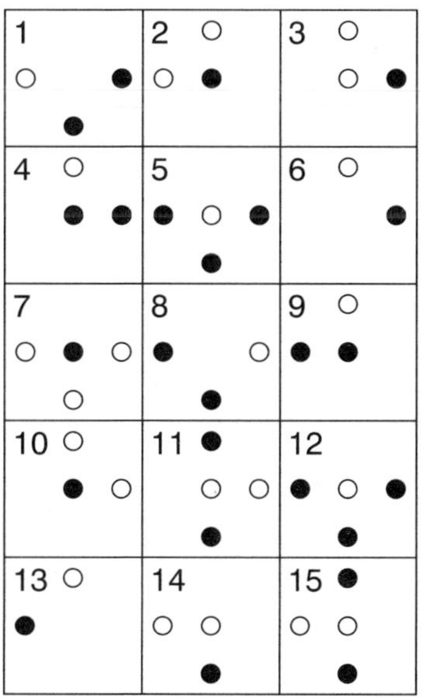

18. Which of the following is not an anagram of an animal?

one leapt   take choir   the plane   trap hen   leg laze

19. Out of 100 women surveyed leaving Harrods, 83 had a white bag, 77 had black shoes, 62 carried an umbrella and 95 wore a ring. What is the minimum number of women who must have had all four items?

20. 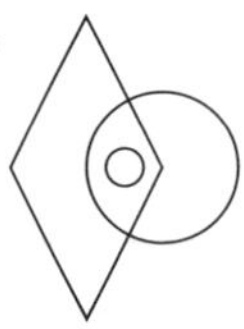

is to

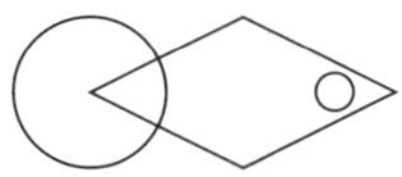

as

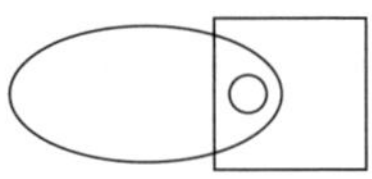

is to

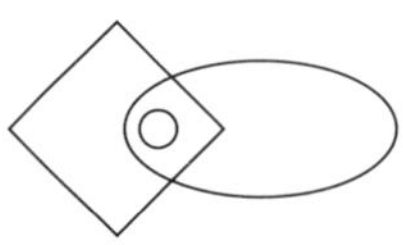

A

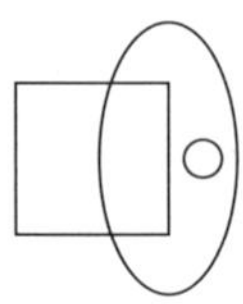

B

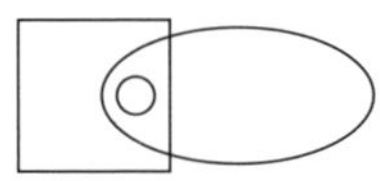

C

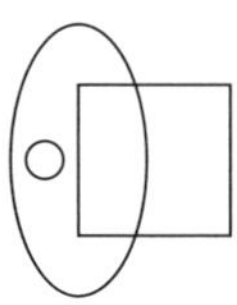

D

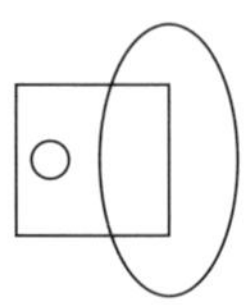

E

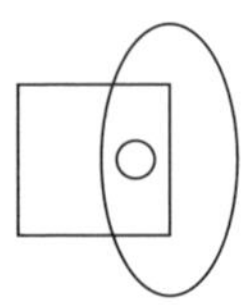

F

21.

3	2	2	3	3	?
4	6	6	6	2	?
7	8	7	8	8	?
5	3	5	5	7	?
1	4	4	1	5	?

What numbers should replace the question marks?

22. Fill in the blanks to make an 11-letter word.

– – – D E M O N – – –

23. Which word means the opposite of PLEBEIAN?

a. vulgar;

b. smooth;

c. glossy;

d. patrician.

24. Place three two-letter bits together to equal a FLOWER.

CR CH OS

ID OC OR

25. Find a word in the brackets that means the same as the two words outside the brackets.

BARREN LAND (– – – – – –) RUN AWAY

26. Find the value of the question mark.

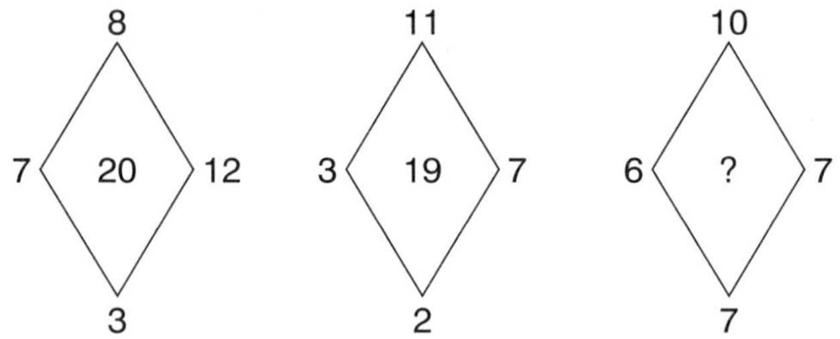

27. Fill in the blanks to find two words that are SYNONYMS (clockwise or anticlockwise).

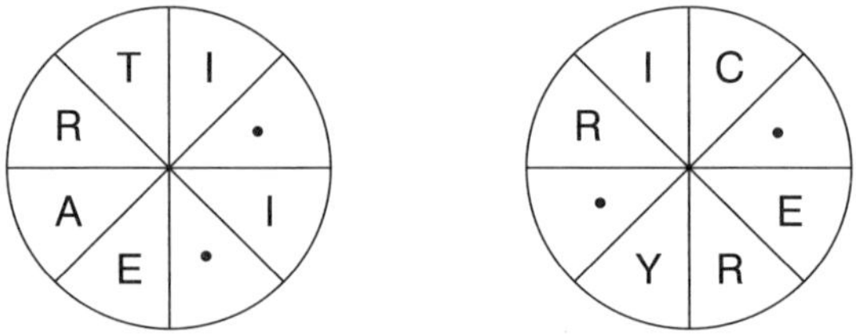

28. Insert a word that completes the first word and starts the second word.

CHAIN (– – – –) MAN

29. Find a word in the brackets that means the same as the two words outside the brackets.

SMALL ARCTIC MAMMAL (– – – – –) BLACK COLOUR

30. Letters are traced across the circle by chords. If the next letter is four letters or less away it will be found by tracing around the circumference.

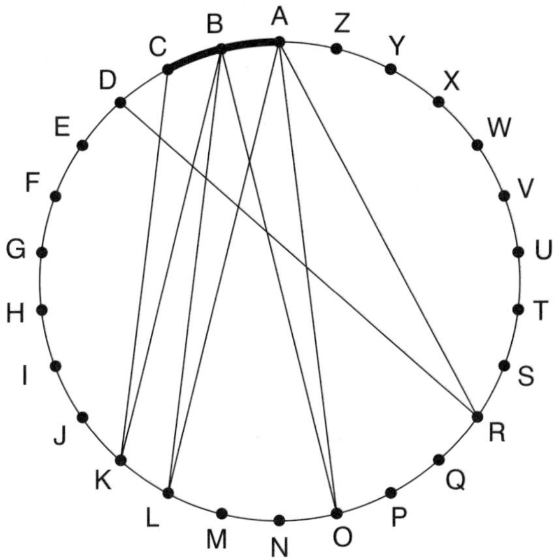

Clue: FOUND IN SCHOOL

31. What number should replace the question mark in the set of analogies below?

352 : 30

296 : 108

628 : ?

32.

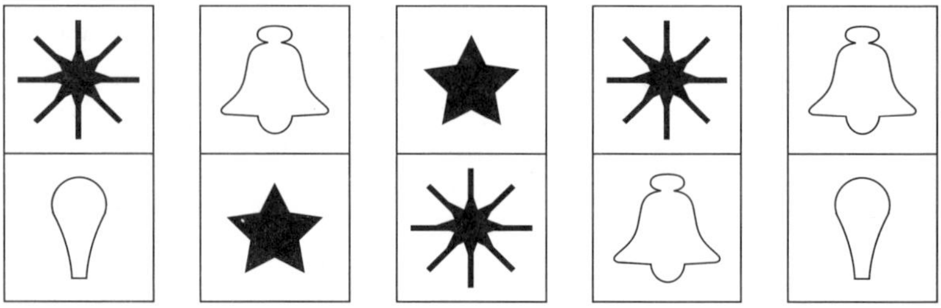

Which figure completes the above set?

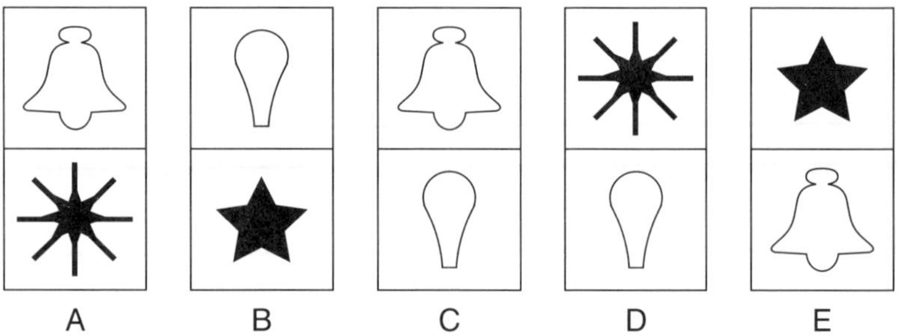

33. Find a one-word anagram for BIAS BULL.

34. some, book, cart, made

Which word below can join the list of the above four words?

part, time, dip, clap or nose

35. What is a quadriga?

a. a printer's block; b. a 4th power of a million;

c. a square dance; d. an ancient chariot;

e. something consisting of four algebraic terms.

36. Which two words are similar in meaning?

INCITE INGENUOUS CULPABLE OVERCOME
HUMANE SUBJUGATE BENIGN INNOCUOUS

37. What word can be prefixed to these words to make new words?

CAVE GO JUNCTION SERVE VEX

38. What is the answer to this sum in decimals?

$$\frac{9}{11} \div \frac{18}{33} \div \frac{50}{10} = x$$

39. irreverent is to disrespectful as indecorous is to:

blasphemous, improper, insulting, vulgar, discourteous

40

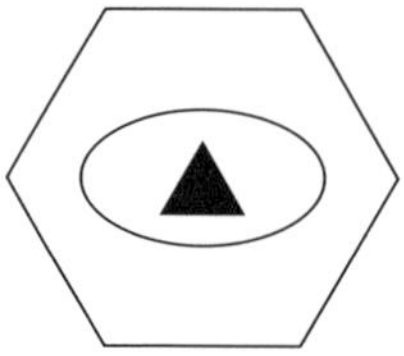

is to

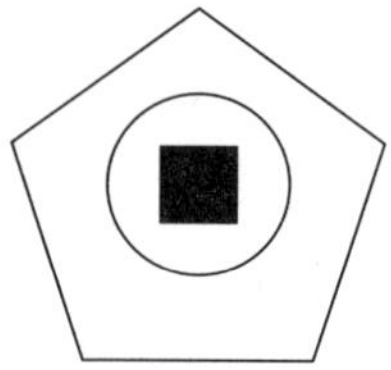

as

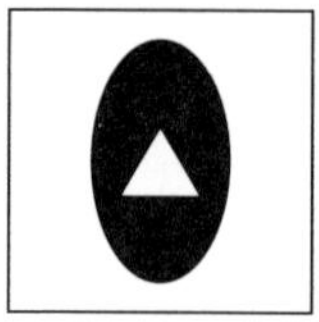

is to

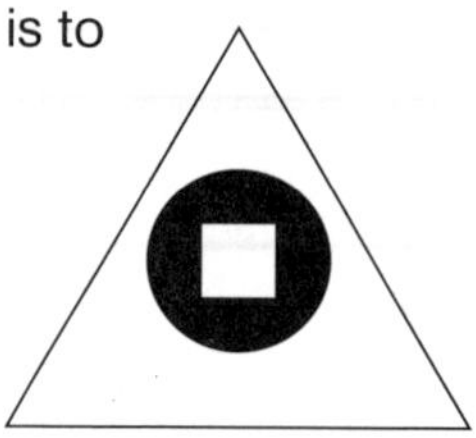

A

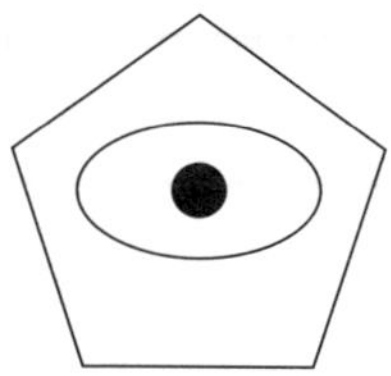

B

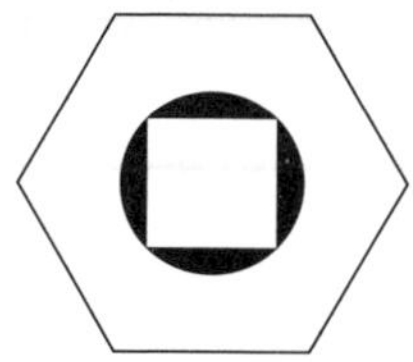

C

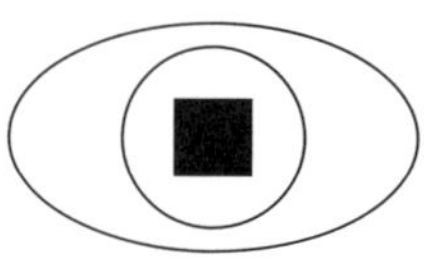

D

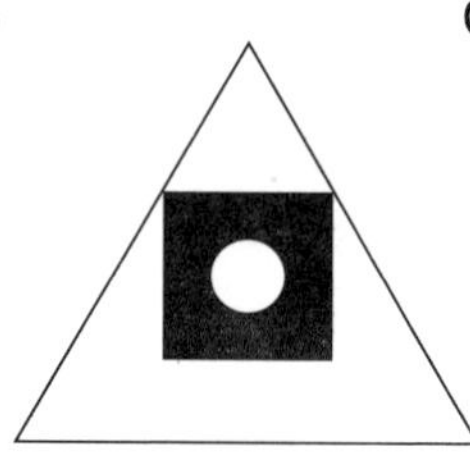

E

Test Eight: Answers

1. 5: each number represents the number of times that a number is adjacent to it, either horizontally, vertically or diagonally.

2. B: the contents of the third hexagon in each row and column are determined by the contents of the first two hexagons. Only when lines appear once in the same position in these two hexagons are they carried forward to the third hexagon.

3. ADORE, CHERISH, VENERATE, REVERE

4. WITH ONE FELL SWOOP

5. E: work along the top row, then back along the second row etc, repeating the first three symbols.

6. OPPOSITE MATCHING

7. MUYJP = jumpy

8. 50 minutes

9. A: looking across and down, only when the same colour dot appears in the same position in the first two hexagons is it carried forward to the third hexagon, but then changes from white to black and vice versa.

10. fanlight: it is an British-English term, the rest are American-English terms.

11. F

12. 7 and 9: the numbers at the bottom are the sum of the digits of the connected numbers at the top.

13. C: the taller triangle remains stationary. The other triangle moves from right to left by half the distance of the base of the taller triangle each time. The section common to both triangles is always shaded.

14. breastbone

15. PENINSULA

16. Tony 42, Cherie 38, Gordon 56

17. 7: all the rest have a mirror-image pairing.

18. artichoke = take chair. The animals are antelope = one leapt, elephant = the plane, panther = trap hen and gazelle = leg laze.

19. 17: add the number of items together, which gives 83 + 77 + 62 + 95 = 317 among 100 women. This gives three items to each and four items to 17 of these women. The least number of women to have all three items is, therefore, 17.

20. B: The square moves from right to left, the ellipse rotates 90 degrees and goes from left to right and the dot moves to the extreme right within the ellipse.

21. From top to bottom: 6 8 7 1 4: in each pair of columns reverse the numbers and add 1 to the odd numbers, but deduct 1 from the even numbers.

22. PANDEMONIUM

23. d. patrician

24. ORCHID

25. DESERT

26. 11:

$7 \times 8 = 56$	$11 \times 3 = 33$	$10 \times 6 = 60$
$3 \times 12 = 36$	$2 \times 7 = 14$	$7 \times 7 = 49$
$56 - 36 = 20$	$33 - 14 = 19$	$60 - 49 = 11$

27. ARTIFICE TRICKERY

28. MAIL

29. SABLE

30. BLACKBOARD

31. 96: $6 \times 2 \times 8$

32. B: it completes every possible pairing of the four different symbols.

33. SILLABUB

34. clap: all can be prefixed by the word hand.

35. d. an ancient chariot

36. SUBJUGATE OVERCOME

37. CON

38. $\frac{9}{11} \times \frac{33}{18} \times \frac{10}{50} = 0.3$

39. improper

40. A: the number of sides of the figure on the outside reduces by one. The figure in the middle changes from ellipse to circle and the number of sides of the figure in the centre increases by one.

Test Nine: Questions

1. Which is the odd one out?

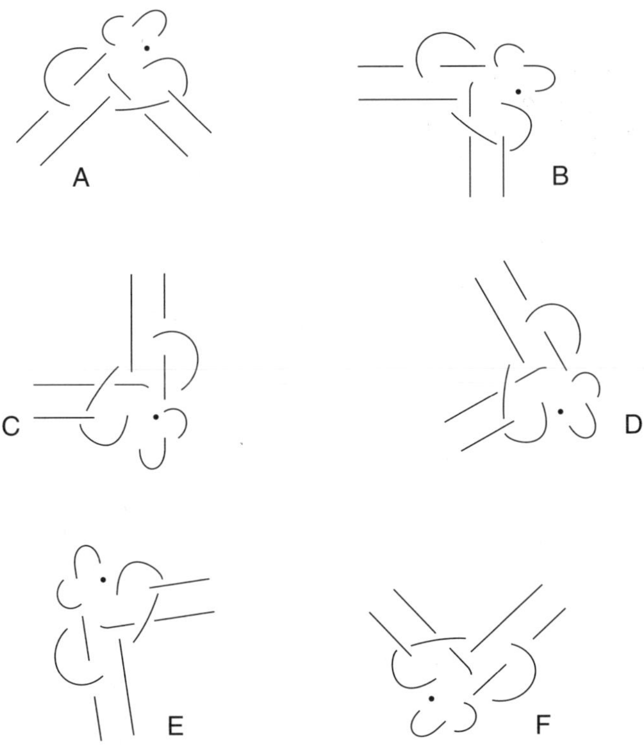

2. female is to nanny as male is to: Joey, Tommy, Harry, Billy, Larry

3. Change one letter only in each word to produce a familiar phrase.

   tin fog cat

4. What number should replace the question mark?

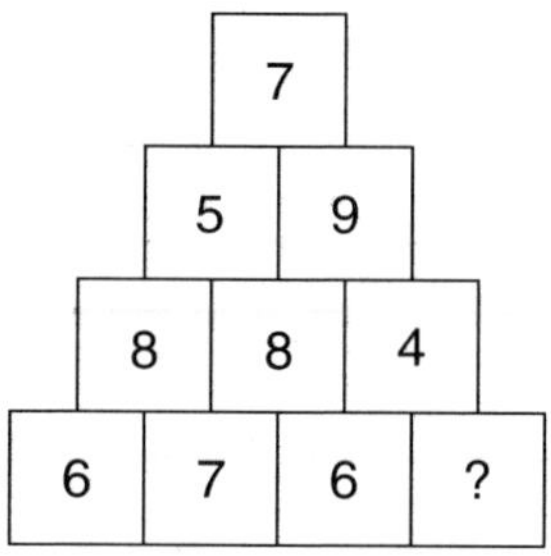

5.

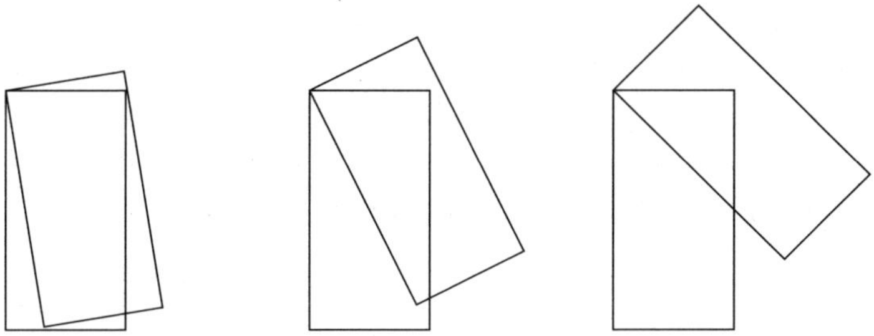

What comes next?

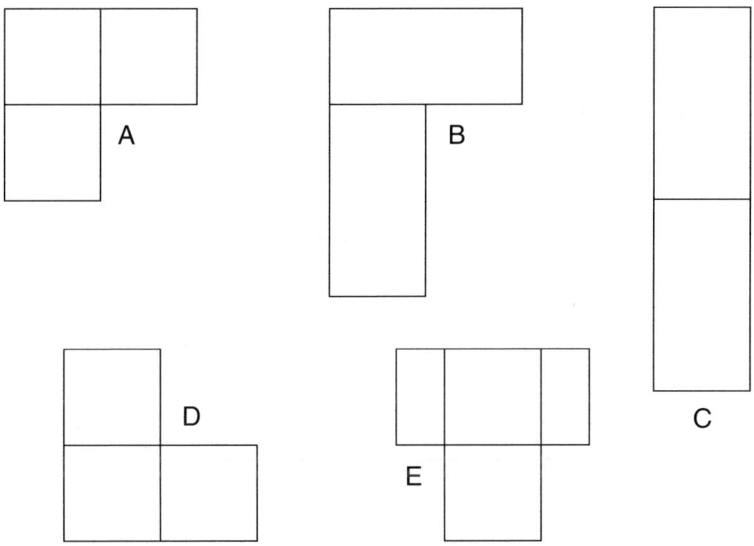

6. Which is the odd one out?

calypso, concerto, aria, shanty, madrigal

7. Insert a word in the brackets that has the same meanings as the definitions either side of the brackets.

ascend (– – – – –) calibration

8. I picked a basket full of apples from my orchard. By the time I arrived home, I had given away 75 per cent to my son, 0.625 of the remainder to my son's neighbour and then eaten one of the remainder. I arrived home with just two apples. How many apples did I originally pick from my orchard?

9. How many lines appear below?

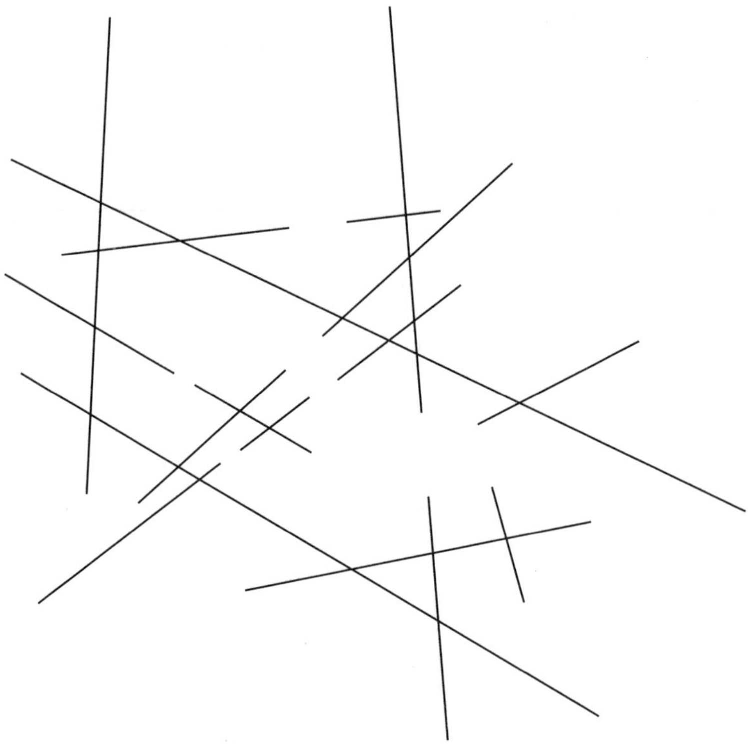

10. Which word in brackets is most opposite in meaning to the word in capitals?

KNACK (necessity, surplus, ineptitude, facility, quell)

11. Solve the anagram in brackets (11 letters) to complete the quotation by Frank Crane.

    Your soul (ironic button) to the sum of things is yourself.

12. What number should replace the question mark?

4	2	3	2	5	4
6	7	5	1	7	3
5	1	3	?	6	5

13. Which is the odd one out?

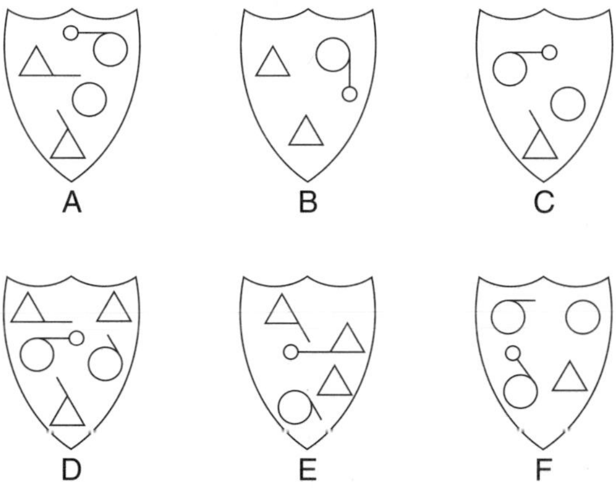

14. Fit the four-letter words into the crossword.

ATOM NOSY COOL LAMP YAWN MAIN SHIP EAST KING

VETO PEAK UNIT DARK ZEST ZEAL UNDO STAG TAKE

TAME SUCH

15. Which four numbers should complete the grid?

2	4	8	3	9	2	4
9	8	3	9	2	4	8
3	4			9	8	3
8	2			2	3	9
4	9	3	8	4	9	2
2	9	3	8	4	2	4
3	8	4	2	9	3	8

16.

Which is the missing segment?

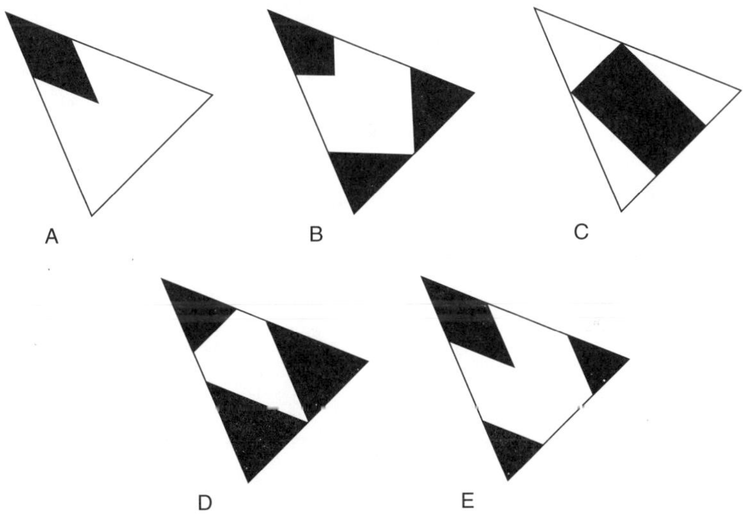

17. Place a word in the bracket that creates another word or phrase when tacked onto the end of the first word, and creates another word or phrase when placed in front of the second word.

stone (– – – –) feet

18. What numbers should go on the bottom line?

3 6 9 15

8 2 10 12

11 8 19 27

19 10 29 39

? ? ? ?

19. Which two words are closest in meaning?

coquetry, flippancy, apathy, adaptability, levity, celerity

20.

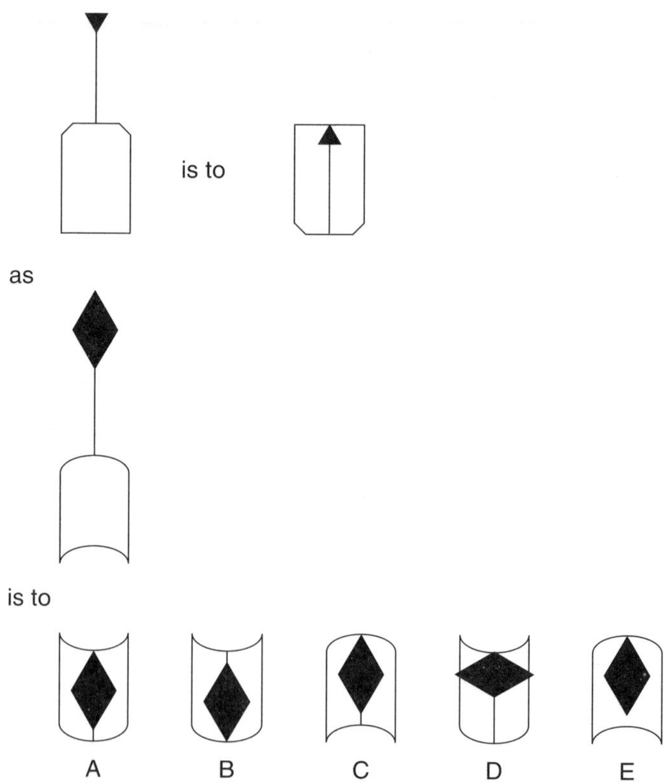

21. Fill in the blanks to find a BOAT (clockwise or anti-clockwise).

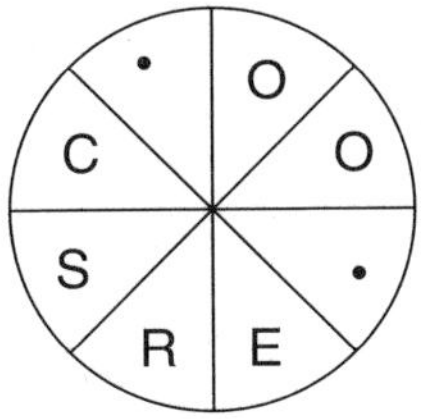

22. What number should replace the question mark?

3624 : 96

2816 : 74

2032 : ?

23. Starting at a corner, spiral in to find a nine-letter word.

H	L	R
S	Y	O
I	U	G

24. What weight must be placed at ? to balance the scale?

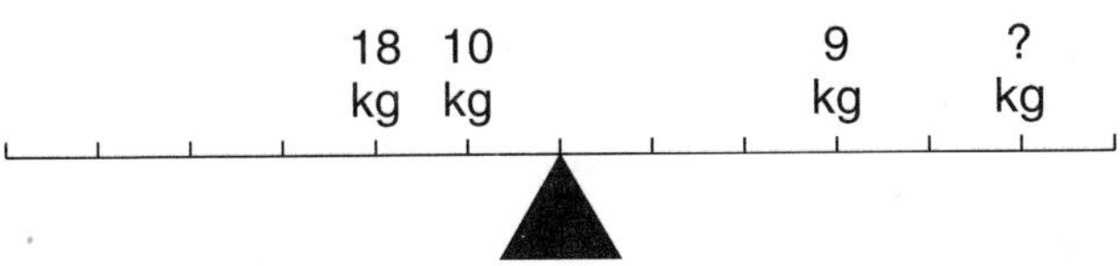

25. What is the answer to this sum in decimals?

$$\frac{18}{99} \div \frac{2}{11} \div \frac{9}{1} = x$$

26. Place four two-letter bits together to equal a BIRD.

CO OR TO AT

OO RO CK AT

27. What is the meaning of PERNICIOUS?

a. destructive;

b. fine judgement;

c. obvious;

d. singular;

e. qualifying.

28. 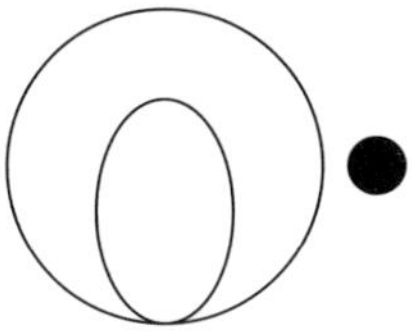 is to 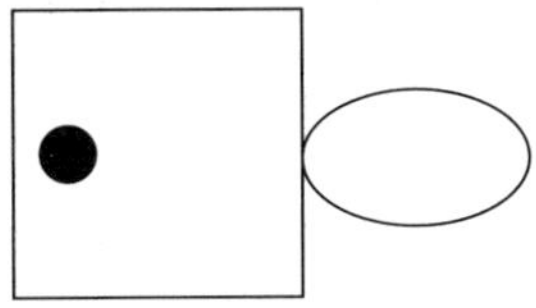

as

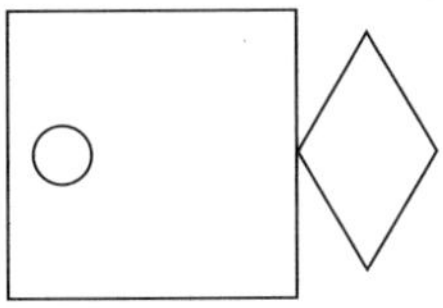

is to

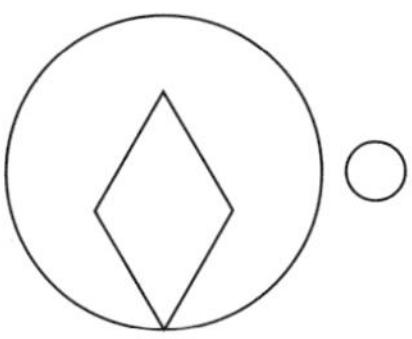
A

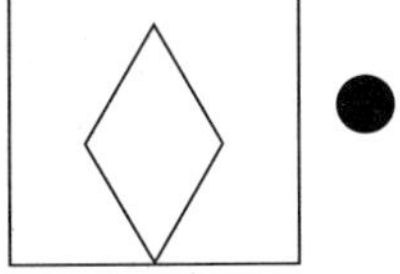
B

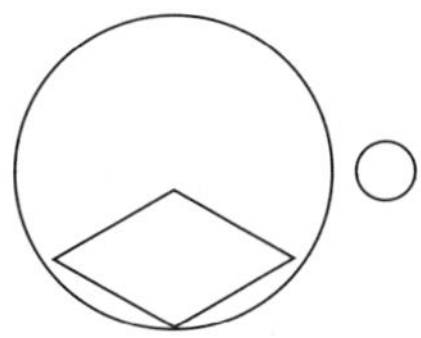
C

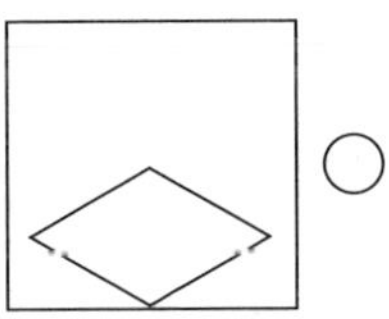
D

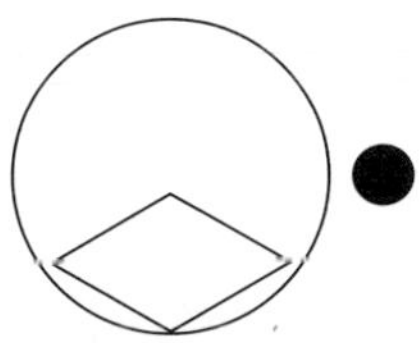
E

29. A well-known phrase has had its vowels removed and the remaining consonants, although appearing in the correct order, have been split into groups of three. What is the phrase?

LTT HCT TFT HBG

30. fuselage is to body as aileron is to: fin, cockpit, wing, tail, rudder

31. What number should replace the question mark?

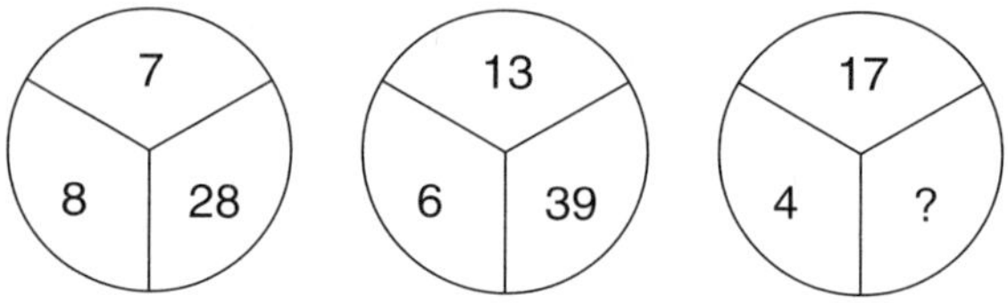

32. What number should replace the question mark?

17, 30, 18¼, 26¼, 19½, 22½, 20¾, 18¾, ?

33. Find a word in the brackets that means the same as the two words outside the brackets.

seed vessel (– – –) group of seals

34. What number should replace the question mark?

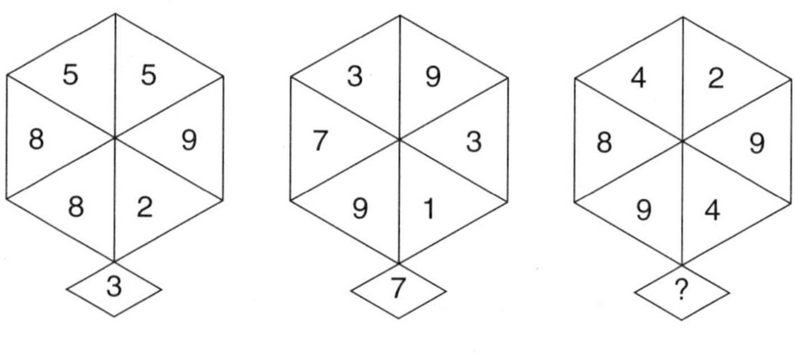

35. What is the value of the question mark?

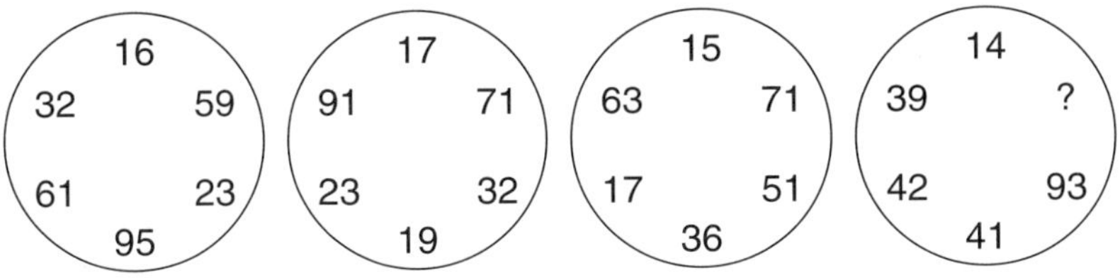

36. Insert a word that completes the first word and starts the second word

HOT (– – –) BELLIED

37. What is the value of x?

$17, 36, 19\frac{1}{2}, 31\frac{3}{4}, 22, 27\frac{1}{2}, 24\frac{1}{2}, 23\frac{1}{4}, x$

38. Complete the three-letter words to find an 11-letter word that is a VEGETABLE.

1st	S	S	E	N	S	O	A	A	S	T	P
2nd	A	P	M	I	K	F	L	D	O	H	E
3rd	•	•	•	•	•	•	•	•	•	•	•

39. Which circle does not contain letters that will make up a word?

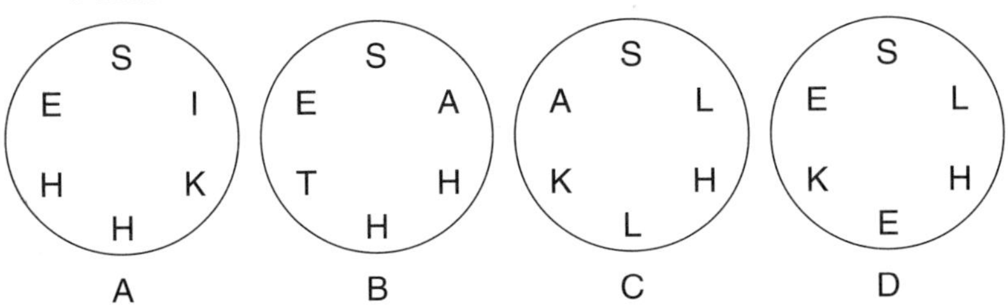

40. Letters are traced across the circle by chords. If the next letter is four letters or less away it will be found by tracing around the circumference.

Clue: LOST THE KEY? (10 letters)

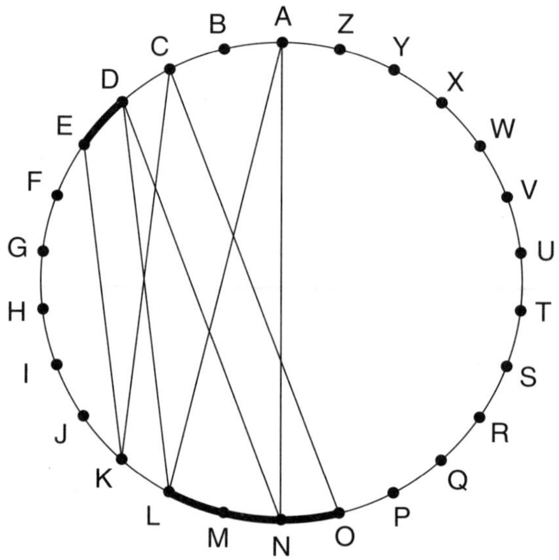

Test Nine: Answers

1. C: all the other figures are identical. In C the dot is in the wrong place.

2. Billy

3. tit for tat

4. 11: each pyramid of three numbers totals 21.

5. B: one rectangle remains stationary while the other rotates by half of the length of the stationary rectangle anticlockwise at each stage.

6. concerto: it is music written for instruments, the rest being songs, typically with words.

7. scale

8. 32: (32 less 75 per cent = 8, less 0.625 = 3, less 1 = 2)

9. 17

10. ineptitude

11. contribution

12. 2: the numbers surrounding each dot are always in ascending/descending order eg, 2467 or 7642.

13. E: the only one where a tail with a little circle is attached to a triangle.

14.

P	E	A	K	■	Z	E	A	L
■	A	■	I	■	E	■	■	■
■	S	■	N	O	S	Y	■	V
S	T	A	G	■	T	A	M	E
U	■	T	■	■	■	W	■	T
C	O	O	L	■	U	N	D	O
H	■	M	A	I	N	■	A	■
■	■	■	M	■	I	■	R	■
S	H	I	P	■	T	A	K	E

15. 8 3

4 2

Start at the bottom left-hand square and work round the perimeter anticlockwise spiralling into the centre and repeating the numbers 38429.

16. D: so that looking round the octagon at segments in pairs, there are four identical pairs with black/white reversal.

17. cold

18. 30 18 48 66. Starting at the top, add pairs of numbers in each column to arrive at the next number.

19. flippancy, levity

20. A: the top and bottom figures fold down and up onto the line respectively.

21. SCHOONER

22. 58: divide each pair of numbers by 4, thus $20 \div 4 = 5$ and $32 \div 4 = 8$

23. ROGUISHLY

24. 4.75.

	LH	RH
	$18\text{ kg} \times 2 = 36\text{ kg}$	$9\text{ kg} \times 3 = 27\text{ kg}$
	$10\text{ kg} \times 1 = 10\text{ kg}$	$3\frac{4}{5} \times 5 = 19\text{ kg}$
	$36\text{ kg} + 10\text{ kg} = 46\text{ kg}$	$27 + 19 = 46\text{ kg}$

25. $\frac{18}{99} \times \frac{11}{2} \times \frac{1}{9} = 0.111$

26. COCKATOO

27. a. destructive

28. C: the square changes to a circle, the diamond goes inside the circle having rotated 90 degrees and the dot moves outside the circle on the right-hand side.

29. LET THE CAT OUT OF THE BAG

30. wing

31. 34: $(17 \times 4) \div 2$

32. 22: there are two alternating series: $+1\frac{1}{4}$ and $-3\frac{3}{4}$.

33. pod

34. 2: $492 \times 2 = 984$. Similarly, $139 \times 7 = 973$ and $295 \times 3 = 885$.

35. 24: in each circle, there are three pairs of numbers, a number and its digits reversed.

36. POT

37. 27: there are two alternating series: ($+2\frac{1}{2}$) 17, $19\frac{1}{2}$, 22, $24\frac{1}{2}$, 27 and ($-4\frac{1}{4}$) 36, $31\frac{3}{4}$, $27\frac{1}{2}$, $23\frac{1}{4}$

38. S S E N S O A A S T P

A P M I K F L D O H E

C A U L I F L O W E R

39. C: (A = SHEIKH; B = SHEATH; D= SHEKEL)

40. LANDLOCKED

Test Ten: Questions

1. Which is the odd one out?

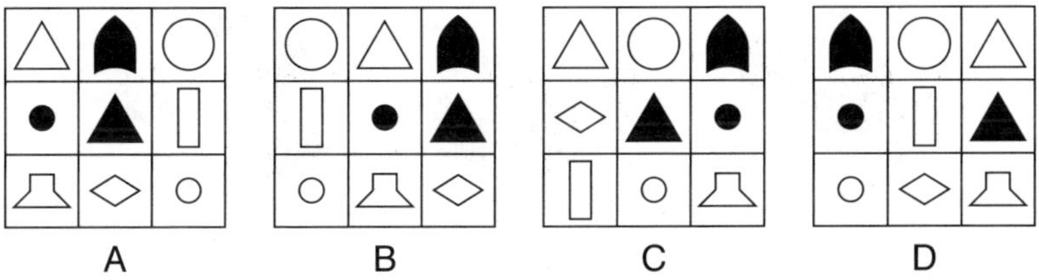

2. Change one letter only in each word to produce a familiar phrase.

   may do fan

3. exigent is to exacting as convoluted is to: esoteric, onerous, elusive, strenuous, intricate

4. What weighs most; something that weighs 60 kg plus one-sixth of its own weight, or something that weighs 46 kg plus one-third of its own weight?

5. 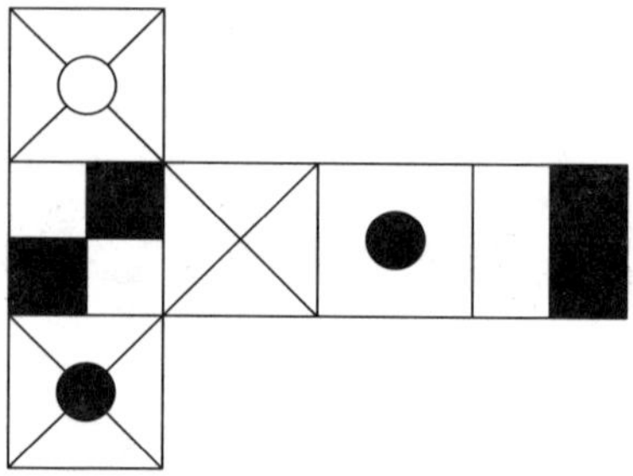

When the above is folded to form a cube, just one of the following can be produced. Which one?

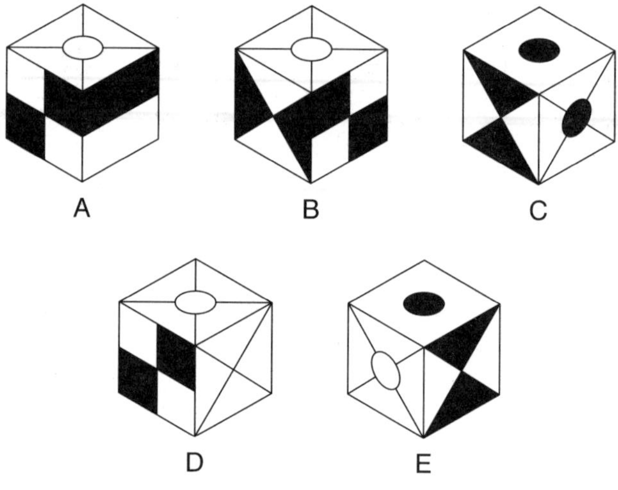

6. Which is the odd one out?

optimize, retrograde, ameliorate, regenerate, enhance

7. What number continues the sequence?

25, 50, 27, 46, 31, 38, 39, ?

8. Insert a word in the brackets that means the same as the definitions either side of the brackets.

protracted (– – – –) desire

9.

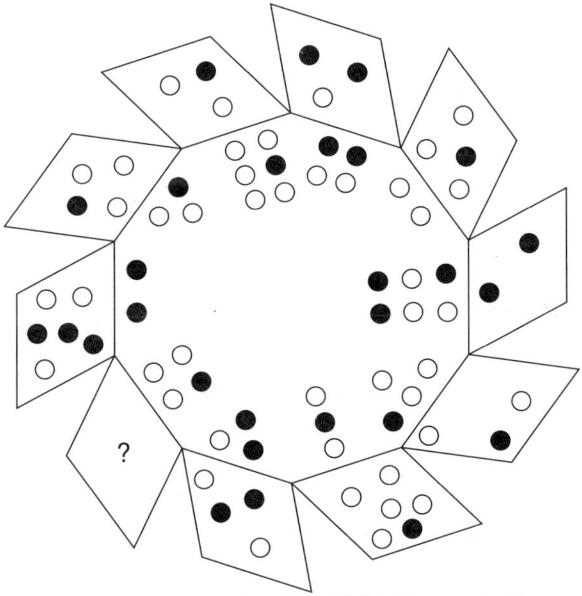

What should replace the question mark?

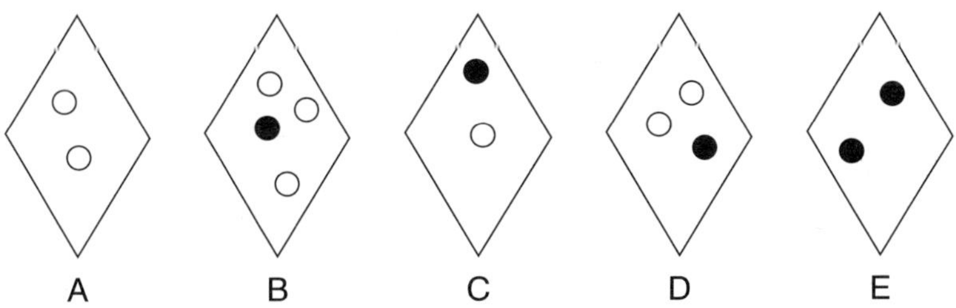

10. What number should replace the question mark?

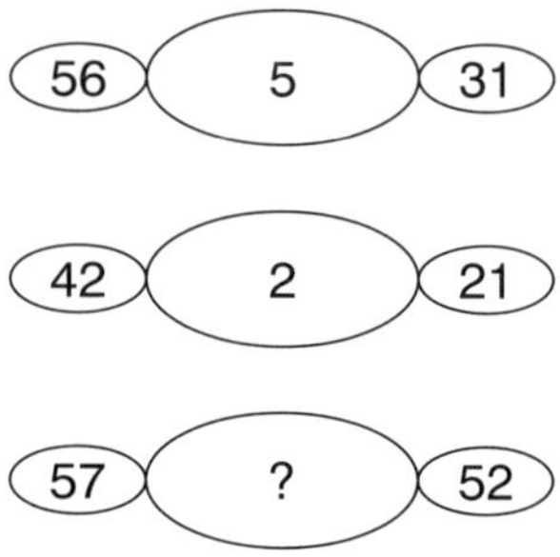

11. What is the longest English word that can be produced from the following 10 letters?

    NURDESBOTA

12. Which word in brackets is closest in meaning to the word in capitals?

    RAMIFICATION (uproar, regulation, collision, consequence, stronghold)

13. Which is the odd one out?

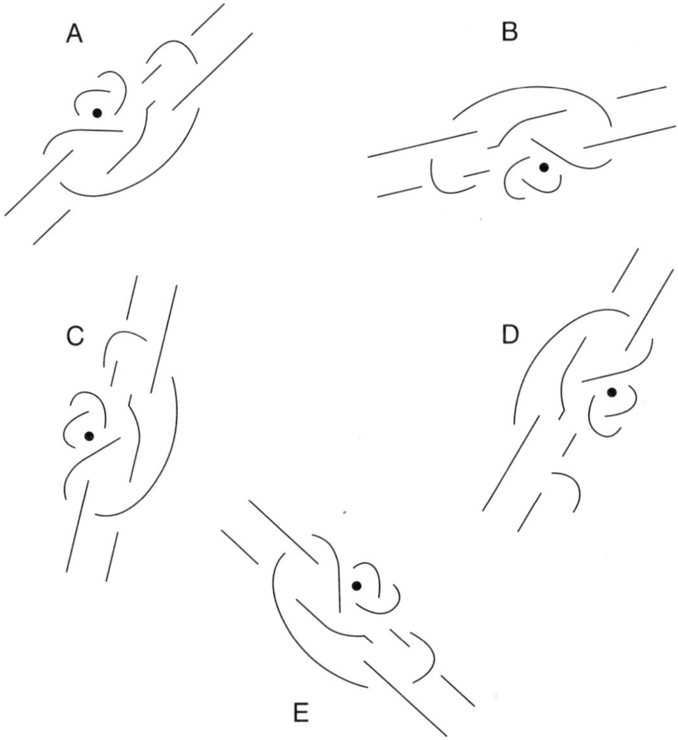

14. What number should replace the question mark?

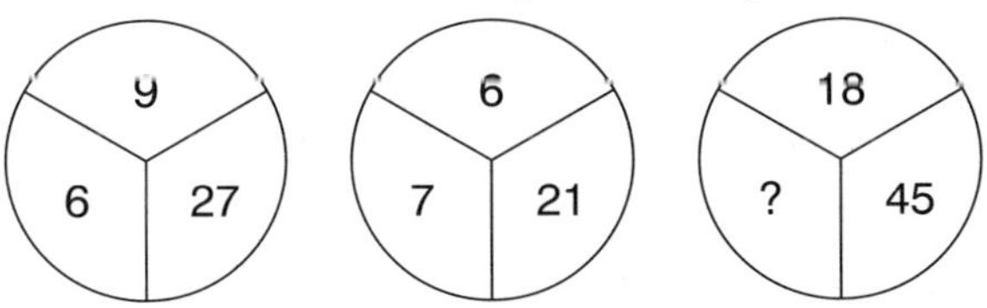

15. Place a word in the bracket that creates another word or phrase when tacked onto the end of the first word, and creates another word or phrase when placed in front of the second word.

march (– – – –) master

16. 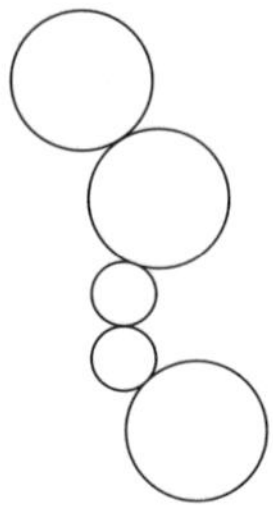

is to 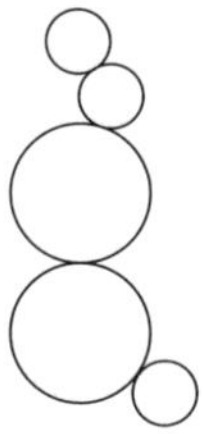

as 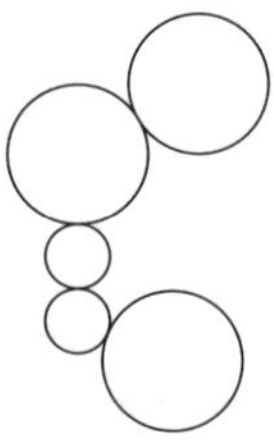

is to

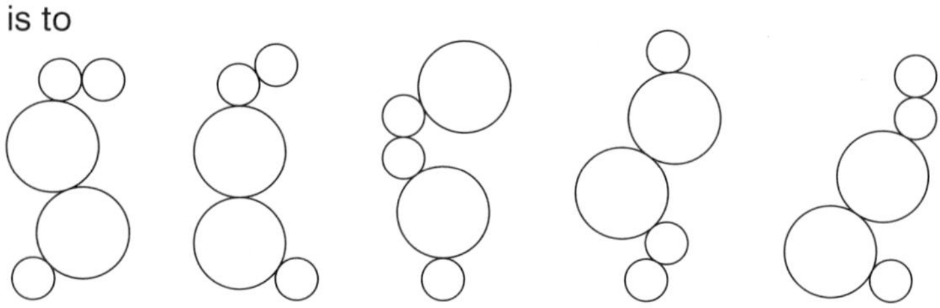

A B C D E

17. What number should replace the question mark?

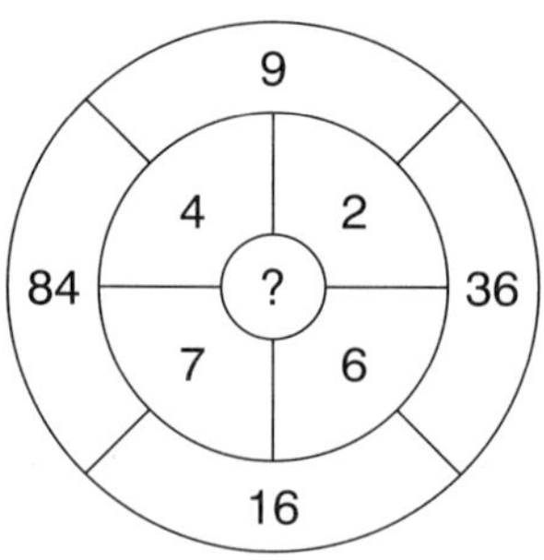

18. UNMARKED SEATS is an anagram of which familiar phrase (four, two, seven letters)?

    Clue: sharp

19. Which two of these words are most opposite in meaning?

    quaint, allegorical, excellent, factual, bellicose, overt

20. Which is the odd one out?

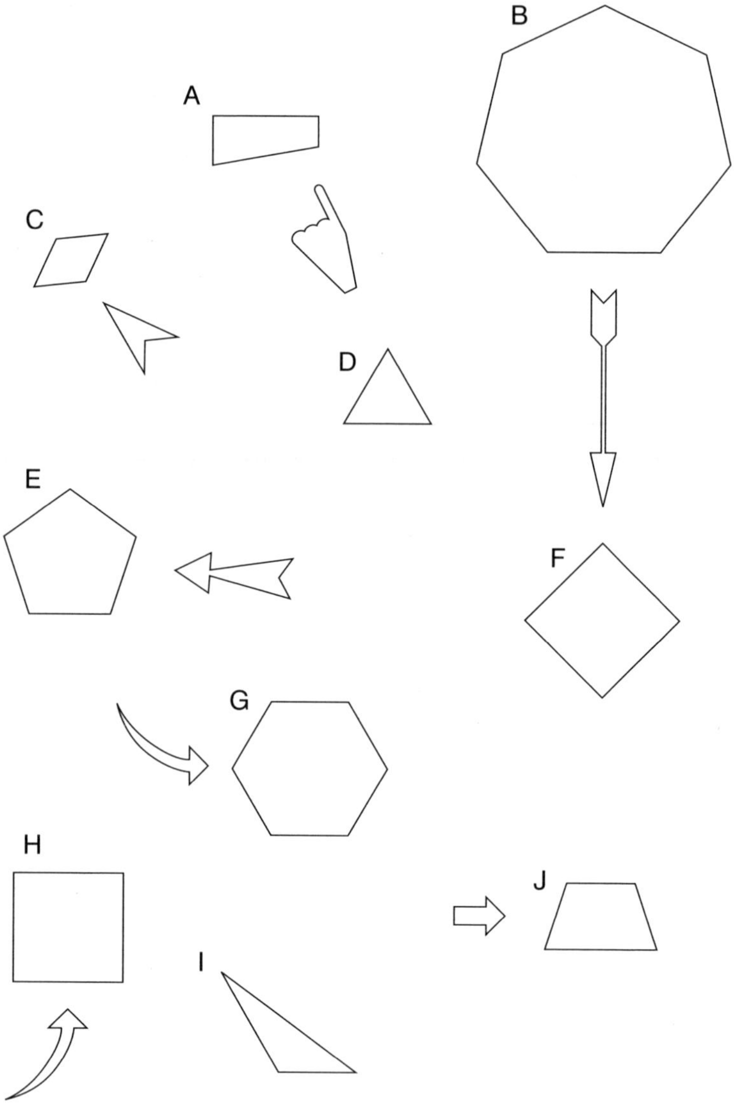

21. Arrange the letters to find two birds

B E E D

O L I N

R R T T

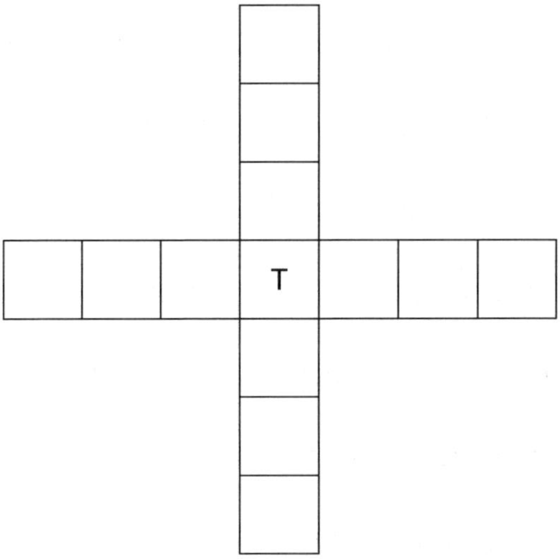

22. Starting at a corner, spiral in to find a nine-letter word.

R	E	V
O	N	E
I	S	R

23. What number should replace the question mark?

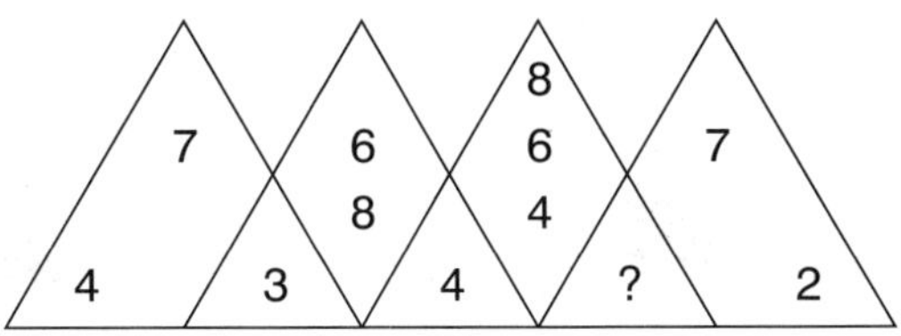

24. Which two words are the most opposite in meaning?

ENFRANCHISE INCITE INCEPTIVE BEAUTIFY

DELINQUENT ABSORB ENSLAVE

25. Which two words are most similar in meaning?

DUPLICITY IMPLY MANIFEST

REPEAT IMPART COVETOUS

IMPORT SERIOUS

26. Which is the odd one out?

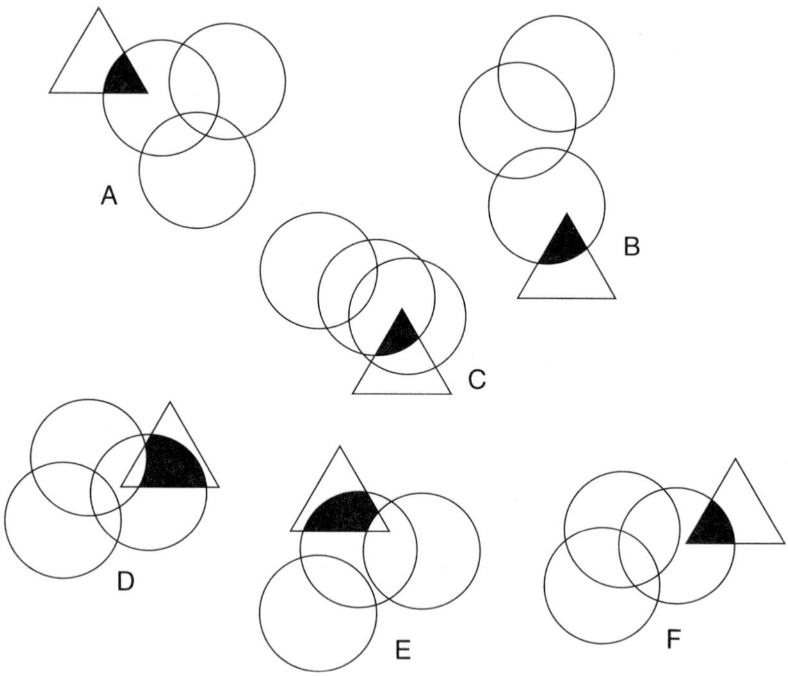

27. What is the lowest odd number and what is the highest square number?

81	27	31	71
64	12	36	30
41	17	26	19
57	37	16	49
25	40	41	42

28. Find the value of the question mark.

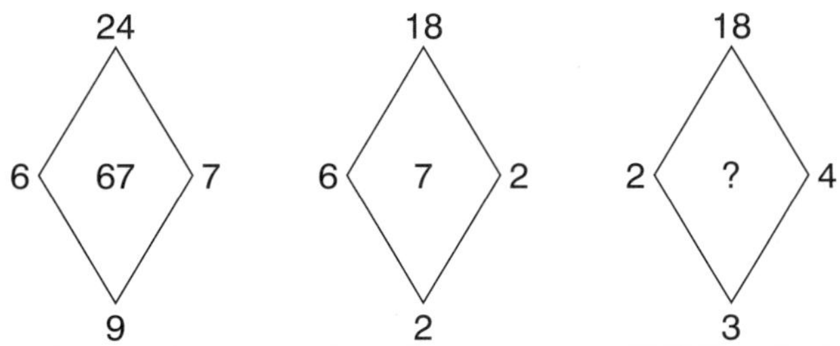

29. Insert a word that completes the first word and starts the second word.

CHARGE (– – – –) SOME

30.

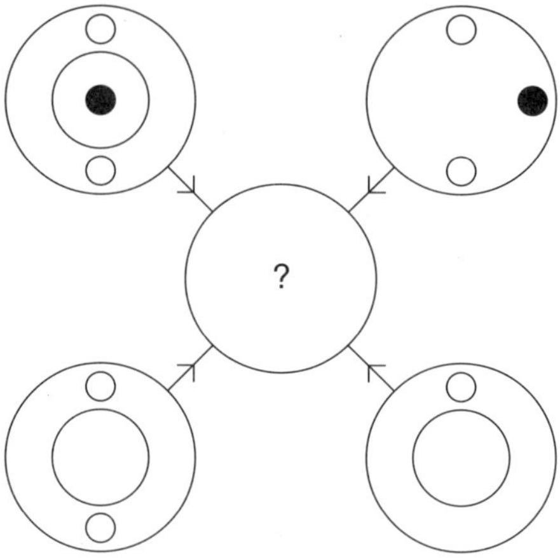

Each line and symbol that appears in the four outer circles above is transferred to the centre circle according to these rules:

If a line or symbol occurs in the outer circles:

once: it is transferred;

twice: it is possibly transferred;

three times: it is transferred;

four times: it is not transferred.

Which of the circles A, B, C, D or E shown below should appear at the centre of the diagram above?

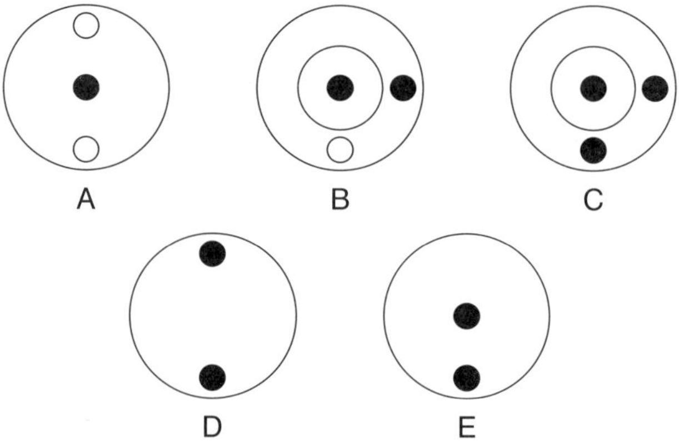

31. What weight should be placed at ? to balance the scales?

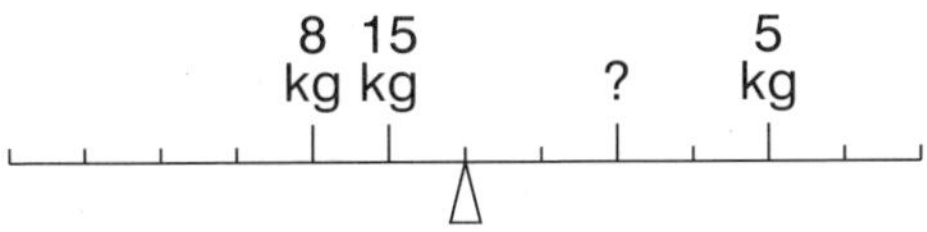

32. Which is the odd one out?

a. TYMBAL;

b. LETITIA;

c. DESCANT;

d. VOLATA;

e. HAUTBOY.

33. Place two three-letter bits together to equal a MINERAL.

SUN GRA LIN

KAO GYP NIT

34. Find a word in the brackets that means the same as the two words outside the brackets.

protrude lips (– – – –) sea fish

35. Place letters in the second line to make the third line spell an occupation.

1st	C	S	B	P	R	T	S
2nd	A	P	E	E	O	O	I
3rd							

36. What is the value of x?

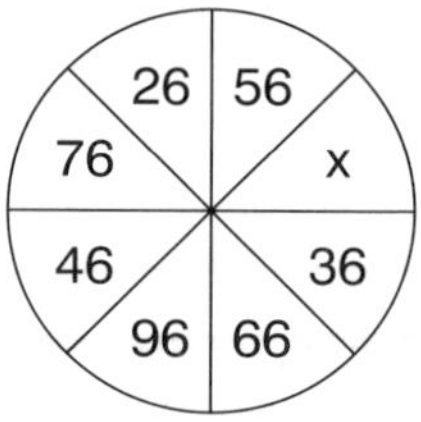

37. Find a word in the brackets that means the same as the two words outside the brackets.

flinch (- - - - -) bird

38. Visit each circle once only to spell out a 10-letter word.

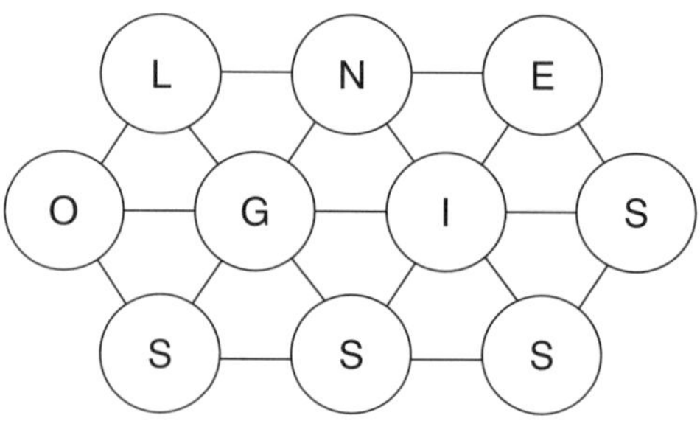

39. flaccid is to limp as friable is to: ductile, soft, flexible, crumbly

40\. Letters are traced across the circle by chords. If the next letter is four letters or less away it will be found by tracing around the circumference.

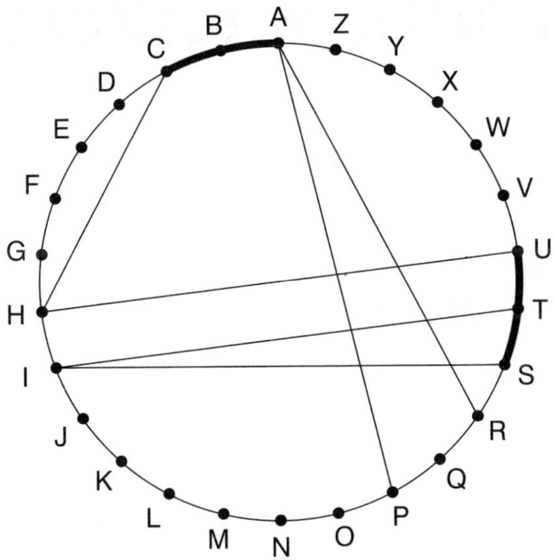

Clue: DOWN TO EARTH (11 letters)

Test Ten: Answers

1. C: in all the others each line across in the same position in each square contains the same three symbols, albeit in a different order.

2. man to man

3. intricate

4. 60 kg + one-sixth of its own weight = 72 kg; 46 kg + one-third of its own weight = 69 kg (ie, 69/3 = 23)

5. D

6. retrograde: it means to worsen, the rest being to improve.

7. 22 : there are two alternate sequences, the first increases by 2, 4, 8 etc and the second decreases by 4, 8, 16 etc.

8. long

9. A: the combination of dots on the inside is the same as in the diamond directly opposite.

10. 3: reverse the numbers either side and divide. So, 75 (57) ÷ 25 (52) = 3.

11. EASTBOUND

12. consequence

13. D: all the others are identical. D contains a line in the wrong position.

14. 5: 5 × 18 = 90. 90 ÷ 2 = 45. Similarly 7 × 6 = 42. 42 ÷ 2 = 21.

15. past

16. B: it contains the same shape of string but with large/small circle reversal.

17. 3: the numbers in the outside ring, top and bottom are arrived at by adding i.e. 4 + 2 + 3 = 9 and 7 + 6 + 3 = 16. The numbers in the outside ring left and right are arrived at by multiplying ie, 4 × 7 × 3 = 84 and 2 × 6 × 3 = 36.

18. keen as mustard

19. allegorical, factual

20. E: the only one where an arrow points to a figure that has an odd number of sides.

21. DOTTREL BITTERN

22. REVERSION

23. 9: the numbers at the bottom are the difference between the sum of numbers in the sections either side. Thus (8 + 6 + 4) – (2 + 7) = 9

24. ENFRANCHISE ENSLAVE

25. IMPLY, IMPORT

26. C: in all the others only the overlapping portion between the triangle and one circle is shaded. In C the portion shaded appears in two circles.

27. 17 and 81

28. 21:

$24 \div 6 = 4$	$18 \div 6 = 3$	$18 \div 2 = 9$
$7 \times 9 = 63$	$2 \times 2 = 4$	$4 \times 3 = 12$
$4 + 63 = 67$	$3 + 4 = 7$	$12 + 9 = 21$

29. HAND

30. B

31. 5.5 kg

LH		RH	
	15 kg × 1 = 15 kg		5 kg × 4 = 20 kg
	8 kg × 2 = 16 kg		5.5 kg × 2 = 11 kg
	15 kg + 16 kg = 31 kg		20 kg + 11 kg = 31 kg

32. b. LETITIA (girl's name). The others are all MUSICAL TERMS.

33. KAOLIN

34. POUT

35.

C	S	B	P	R	T	S
A	P	E	E	O	O	I
M	A	T	A	D	O	R

36. 86: start at 26 and increase by 10 every three segments in a clockwise motion.

37. quail

38. GLOSSINESS

39. crumbly

40. PARACHUTIST